Never Stop

Teaching and Leading
Help heal our nation

Herbert I. Burns Jr.

CONTENTS

Preface

There is never a more important time in your life than now. There is never a more important time in our nation than now. Our nation needs healing now. You are the remedy to help heal our nation through your teaching and leading. The author takes you on a historical journey from the founding of our republic to the unwell times our nation is now in. He creates a prescription of progress for you if you are willing to take and make the stand with your teaching and leadership to help heal our nation.

The prescription involves your children, your families, your faith, and work. All of these were the healthy foundations of our republic. The author also provides you with the opportunity to fill in the blanks as our future evolves. Will our nation become healthier or sicker? It is up to you. Continue reading for the full diagnosis and remedy. You can make a change in our nation's future. Start now before our republic dies, and spread the word to others as we help to heal our nation!

CHAPTER ONE

July 4th

Never stop teaching and leading. Keep America great! As an educator for over 40 years in higher education and my wife, Susan, an elementary schoolteacher for 40 years, we bring almost 100 years of teaching and seeing what is happening in our educational structures in America today. We see the dumbing down and exclusion of certain parts in our past educational system, which is eroding more and more. In today's time we are teaching to the test. High school and elementary schools are teaching to "The Test." It's not about real education, it's about meeting the standards of the "The Test." Let me say this another way. When I was teaching in college, I would make the test for my students to take. I knew the content for my course, and I also knew the important questions to ask that would allow me to evaluate the knowledge the students had retained in order to progress to the next level class. I did not have someone give me a standardized test for my class. One size does not fit all. Someone in another state does not know the technical skills required for my students in my employment region. So why should I give them a test that someone else has created. Then I would be teaching to the test! I might teach the class differently than another, but that is what separates good teachers from great teachers and leaders. I challenge you as you continue to read to have an open mind, and that if you are blessed to have an opportunity to teach, you will enlighten, educate, enrich, engage, and empower students to be their best.

Today is July 4th, 2020. Last night I watched and listened to our 45th President, Donald John Trump, address the nation live on TV from Mount Rushmore. Just imagine! Since the founding of this great nation in 1776, over 244 years ago, we have had only 45 presidents to lead our nation through times of turmoil, triumph, and togetherness. My wife and

I were privileged one year to visit this great national park that serves as a historical venue for Americans. I remember as we entered, we could see the avenue of the states. The walkway leading to the entrance was lined with flags on each side of all 50 states. What an amazing reminder this is that we are one nation in union. Better expressed by our Constitution: one nation under God. In the past our states fought for independence from Britain. In the past our states fought for independence from slavery. In the past our states fought wars in other countries for the independence and freedoms of others. We are a republic governed by the people, which we must never forget! Let our voices be heard when we are no longer represented by those we have elected. But let us be certain that those we elect will represent and uphold the great Constitution of these United States.

While we were at Mount Rushmore, we had the rare opportunity to meet and talk with the last living worker of the monument there, Donald "Nick" Clifford. What an honor to actually meet someone who dedicated many years of his life helping to create a monument to be a forever reminder of our history and heritage. Nick was only 17 years old when he started work at Mount Rushmore. He was in his 90s when we talked with him.

President Trump reminds us of the importance of our great nation and the significance of protecting the heritage of our history. To do this we must Never Stop Teaching and Leading. Keep America great. Take a moment and look at the cover of this book. Our first lesson comes from here. There are four things that I want you to notice and think about.

First, the American flag. Men and women have fought and died while carrying this flag into battle to protect and serve us as the republic of the United States. This flag is the most important symbol of these United States. Do our students really know about its symbolism? When we started as nation, we were only 13 colonies. There are thirteen stripes on our flag representing those founding colonies. Those white strips symbolize purity and innocence. The red strips represent hardness and valor, and I would go further to say it represents the blood shed to protect our great nation. Then there are the 50 stars on a field of blue. But remember that our first flag only had 13. How amazing that this field of stars has grown to 50 now, which celebrates the growth and representation of this great nation. Finally, those stars are set on a field of blue. The field of blue represents perseverance, vigilance, and justice. Anyone that would burn or desecrate our great flag are destroying our history, our nation, the symbol of our freedoms, and justice. This brings harm to us as a nation. How have we as a nation educated our young to be so disrespectful of their freedoms and liberties? Where is truth in dialogue? Why has destruction of others' property become the symbolic dialogue that implies I will destroy you if you do not do what I want. I will shame you if you do not agree with my point of view! The simplest way to describe this is sinful acts against God, and country.

Second is an image of our nation's capitol. The

house of we the people. From the Constitution of the United States we have this preamble.

"We the People of the United States, in Order to form a more perfect Union, establish Justice, insure domestic Tranquility, provide for the common defense, promote the general Welfare, and secure the Blessings of Liberty to ourselves and our Posterity, do ordain and establish this Constitution for the United States of America."

Let us never, never forget what our representatives in this great house are supposed to do for us, not what they are to do for themselves. Remember this is the home of our represented republic to serve us as a nation.

Third is a silhouette image representing leadership. A group of leaders are extending a helping hand to lift someone of the hurdle at that moment in their life. We all need to be the right kind of leaders, and as you read further in the book, those teaching and leading moments will come forward hopefully as an inspiration to others.

Fourth, look for the cross in the clouds. We must never forget the Judeo-Christian values that helped form this nation from our founding fathers. The laws of moral action, equality of all, God- given human rights, separation of church and state. We as a nation must never let government regulate our religion. Sadly, we have let this happen in 2020. It's time to stand up and speak up. We as a nation can no longer be a silent majority. We cannot and must not let the violence of a few dictate our future and erase our past. It's time for us all to be great teachers and leaders now and for our future.

Not only is it important to remember our heritage but it is just as important to teach about it. It is absolutely crazy that in today's times there are people wanting to erase and destroy physical evidence of our past by tearing down structures. They want everyone to conform to their ideological standards, and if you don't then you are called out for being independent. Remember that this is a free nation and that all voices must and can be heard in a civil manner; we are an independent nation. History must not be excluded from our academic environments. We must bring the teaching of American history and our Constitution back into our elementary and high schools. It needs to be something that students are tested on! It is absolutely amazing when you see millennials that are asked simple questions like:

Who is our founding father?

What is the name of the vice president?

What year was our country founded?

What are the three branches of government?

What was the war where we declared our independence?

Some know the answer, but many do not. It still amazes me to this day how little of our American history is taught because it is not required when educators teach to the test. It is time to put education back into the hands of our educators. It is time to reeducate those who are teaching our educators. It is time to teach all truth in education, and not teach just to influence a movement of socialism but a movement of truism in history – the good, the bad, and the ugly, leading to what makes us great as a nation, not what you just want me to believe. If we do not know historically from whence we came, how can we know where we need to go in the future. Have we learned nothing from our past? So here we are in the year 2020.

I think that it would be valuable to look at our past and prepare a list of special people and events in our nation to serve as a starting point in teaching others about this historical picture of America. Some of you may already be aware of such events and activities, but many still have extraordinarily little understanding of them. This will be their starting point. This for them will be a historical marker to look further and to dig deeper into the rich history of our nation. Let us never forget it or try to erase it!

American ancestors and their gifts to us
Historical highlights and their place in our nation

As you begin to review this historical progression, I thought since this is the year 2020 that it might be interesting to break down our historical evolution in 20-year segments starting from 1776. This is a large view of events just to highlight what stands out to me. It serves as a resource to you to share with your children and as an encouragement to look in greater detail at facts and information about our past heritage. From my previous book "Never Stop! Asking, discovering, and sharing!" Please ask, discover, and share as you continue this journey of "Teaching & Leading." Let us begin.

But remember this:
"I like the dreams of the future better than the history of the past." Thomas Jefferson

---

Historical highlights and their place in our nation
1776 – 1796

President
George Washington (the founding father of our nation).

Events
In 1776, the 13 American colonies severed political ties with Great Britain because of taxation without representation. Ties were broken by a Declaration of Independence created through and by the Continental Congress. This eventually led to the start of the Revolutionary War, which did not end until a treaty was signed in Paris, France, in 1783, recognizing the United States of America and its borders. The war lasted for seven years.

Other events to explore during this time:

The French and Indian War; U.S. Ambassadors; signers of the Declaration of Independence; the Declaration of Independence; the Electoral College; republican government.

After the treaty was signed, we were governed for five years by the Articles of the Confederation until 1789 when it was replaced by the U.S. Constitution. The Electoral College was formed, and our first president was elected on April 30, 1789.

Some events as referenced from Wikipedia: Timeline of the United States. For additional information and details, go to Wikipedia.

1785
- The University of Georgia becomes America's first state-chartered university

1790
- First U.S. patent

1791
- First Bank of the United States chartered

1793
- Fugitive Slave Act passed

1794
- Whiskey Rebellion
- Battle of Fallen Timbers
- Eli Whitney invents the cotton gin

1795
- Treaty of Greenville
- 11th Amendment ratified

1796
- Pickney's Treaty; Treaty of Tripoli
- Tennessee becomes the 16th state
- First U.S. presidential election

1797 – 1817

Presidents

John Adams defeats Thomas Jefferson in the U.S. presidential election in 1796 and becomes our second president in 1797. Then Thomas Jefferson followed as the third president, then James Madison as our fourth president.

After winning our independence as a nation, we began to become politically divided over disagreements over the function and purpose of the federal government. These continued into the presidency of Thomas Jefferson and became even worse. During the Jefferson presidency the size of our nation was doubled by the purchase of the Louisiana Territory from France. After the war of 1812, Britain realized even more the existence of the United States as a new independent nation. America began to create a culture uniquely its own and began to expand from the Atlantic to the Pacific.

Events

1797
- Eli Whitney creates interchangeable musket parts

1798
- Alien Sedition Acts (divided political parties for many years)

- Charles Brown early American novelist and historical political writer.

1799
- Fires Rebellion

1799
- Logan Act

1800
- Library of Congress founded

1804
- 12th Amendment ratified
- New Jersey abolishes slavery
- Burr-Hamilton duel
- Lewis and Clark set out northwestern expedition
- Thomas Jefferson reelected president 1807
- Embargo Act
- Robert Fulton invents the steamboat
- U.S. slave trade with Africa ends

1808
- James Madison elected president

1809
- Non-Intercourse Act

1812
- War of 1812
- James Madison recommends National Day of Prayer

1814
- British troops burn Washington, D.C.

1815
- Battle of New Orleans

1816
- James Monroe elected president
- Indiana becomes 19th state

Presidents

James Madison, James Monroe, John Quincy Adams, Andrew Jackson, Martin Van Buren.

Now this nation is beginning a time of reform and expansion. The country is about to expand into a huge territory. This time is also recognized for the disappearance and appearance of political parties, including the Democratic, the Whig, the American, the Free Soil, and the Republican parties. As the nation expanded it also displaced other groups including Native Americans and Mexicans.

Social reforms began to increase, driven by religious revivals. These reforms included temperance, improving care for prisoners, the insane and the poor; creation of a public school system, abolishing slavery, and trying to gain equal rights for women.

Events

1818
- The first separate black denomination of the African Methodist Episcopal Church established

1819
- Jarena Lee becomes first female AME preacher

1820
- Joseph Smith founds Mormonism

1821
- Boston English High School opens; one of the first public high schools in the U.S.

1825
- Erie Canal opens; New York becomes the Empire State

1830
- Electro-magnetic motor invented
- First U.S.-build locomotive

1831
- Reaping machine invented
- William Lloyd Garrison creates the abolitionist newspaper, "The Liberator"

1832
- Disciples of Christ Church founded

1833
- Sewing machine invented

1833
- Threshing machine invented

1835
- Attempted Andrew Jackson assassination

1836
- Battle of the Alamo
- McGuffey Readers is published

1837
- The first Institute of Higher Education for African Americans is founded

1838
- Trail of Tears. Forced removal of the Cherokee Nation from the southeastern United States which led to over 4,000 deaths

1839 – 1859

Presidents

Martin Van Buren, William Henry Harrison, John Tyler, James K. Polk, Zachary Taylor, Millard Fillmore, Franklin Pierce, James Buchanan.

A time in America that saw great expansions to the West, religious groups diversifying and expanding. Victory over the Mexicans, and the beginnings of the great gold rush to the West which contributed to a mass and rapid expansion of western territories. Two presidents die while in office and their VPs become president. More conflicts with Native Americans continue, plus a governmental conflict with the religious group of the Mormons. Finally, towards the end of this period is the raid on Harpers Ferry as an attempt to arm slaves and create conflict for the slave owners. As we can see, this is becoming the spark leading the nation into the Civil War. Technology changes the speed of communication by the invention of the telegraph and the cylinder printing press. All a prelude of what the future holds.

Events

1841
- President Harrison dies after only a month in office
- Vice President Tyler becomes the 10th president

1843
- Attempt to impeach President Tyler fails
- Charles Goodyear perfects vulcanized rubber

1844
- James K. Polk elected the 11th president
- Samuel Morse creates the telegraph

1846
- The Mexican-American War begins

1848
- Treaty of Guadalupe ends the Mexican-American War
- Dred Scott sues for his freedom

1846
- Zachary Taylor becomes the 12th president
- Beginning of the great California Gold Rush
- Cylinder printing press

1850
- President Taylor dies, Vice President Fillmore becomes the 13th President

1852
- Franklin Pierce elected the 14th president after his predecessor Fillmore served only two years

1854
- Whig Party collapses

1856
- Pottawatomie massacre known as "Bleeding Kansas"

1857
- Utah War between the Mormons and the U.S. government
- First financial crisis, the Panic of 1857
- Otis invents the elevator

1858
- Lincoln-Douglas debates

1859
- John Brown's raid on Harpers Ferry first attempt

of a slave rebellion
- First oil well drilled in Pennsylvania

1860 – 1880

Presidents
Abraham Lincoln, Andrew Johnson, Ulysses S. Grant, Rutherford B. Hayes.

These 20 years in American history are reflective of our nation's internal conflicts and its achievements. Lincoln becomes president and leads us to a successful end to the Civil War. Less than one week later he is assassinated. During this time, he freed the slaves and delivered the Declaration of Independence at Gettysburg. Native American Indians are still being driven from their homelands and killed. The Ku Klux Clan is formed by factions of the Democrat Party to try and put down black voting. Technology continues to develop and expand with the creations of the telegraph, Pony Express, Transcontinental Railroad, typewriter, and many other technologies. Now the United States is starting to communicate faster and travel faster, laying the groundwork for the next amazing 20 years in our history.

Events
1860
- Abraham Lincoln becomes the 16th president of the United States
- Beginning of the Pony Express

1861
- Convention to form the Confederate States of America
- Lincoln sworn in as President
- Attack on Fort Sumter
- President Lincoln calls for volunteers to fight the secession of the Confederate States
- U.S. enters into the Civil War

1862
- Dakota war ends. Over 1,000 Dakota Sioux jailed, and 38 Mankato were hanged over late payments of annuities.
- Largest mass execution in U.S. history
- President issues Emancipation Proclamation, stating that all slaves in places of rebellion against the federal government would be free as of January 1, 1863

1863
- Gettysburg address by President Lincoln at Gettysburg

1865
- The Civil War ends
- Abraham Lincoln is assassinated in Ford's Theatre, Washington, D.C.
  - Vice President Andrew Johnson then becomes president
- The Thirteenth Amendment, abolishing slavery, takes effect

1866
- The Civil Rights Act of 1866 is passed by Congress, the first federal law protecting the rights of African Americans

- The Ku Klux Klan forms secretly to discourage African Americans from voting

1867
- First typewriter invented

1868
- Ulysses S. Grant becomes President

1869
- Final golden spike finishes the transcontinental railroad

1870
- The first African American to be sworn into office in the U.S. Congress, Hiram Rhodes Revels
- The 15th Amendment to the Constitution is declared ratified, and African Americans can now vote

1871
- First professional baseball league
- The Great Chicago Fire

1872
- Civil rights restored to citizens of the South
- President Grant reelected
- Susan B. Anthony illegally casts a vote to publicize the cause of women's right to vote

1875
- John McCloskey, the New York archbishop, becomes the first cardinal in the United States named by the papacy
- First Kentucky Derby
- Muslim immigrants arrive in New York
- James Healy becomes first black American Catholic bishop

1876
- Battle of Little Big Horn

1877

•Rutherford B. Hayes becomes president of the U.S.

1878

•First commercial telephone exchange created in Connecticut

1779

•Thomas Edison patents cylinder phonograph

1880

•Construction of the Panama Canal begins by the French and later to be completed by the U.S.

1881 – 1901

Presidents

James A. Garfield, Charles A. Arthur, Grover Cleveland, Benjamin Harrison, Grover Cleveland, William McKinley.

These next 20 years are times of aggression, progression, and regression. Our country engages in many military aggressions to expand and gain control of other territories in the Pacific and the Caribbean. Progression includes the expansion of technologies and transportation. Regression occurs as the Civil Rights Act is overturned. The result is that in the next 20 years, thousands of African Americans would be lynched. A patent for the automobile is granted and a president is shot and later dies from the wounds. Our country is scrambling and dysfunctional in many ways. This time is also noted as the rise of industrial America. America moved from lamps to lights, from horses to cars. The industrial working class grew as did the number of immigrants entering America. This was a time of unforgettable changes.

Events

1881
- Booker T. Washington becomes the leader of the Tuskegee Institute to train African Americans to become teachers
- Sitting Bull surrenders to American troops

1882
- Forty-nine African Americans are known to have been lynched

1883
- Brooklyn Bridge opens
- Five standard time zones established in the U.S.
- Civil Rights Act overturned

1884
- Grover Cleveland becomes president

1886
- The Statue of Liberty dedicated by President Grover Cleveland

1888
- Benjamin Harrison elected President

1889
- The great land rush in America

1890
- The Battle of Wounded Knee, South Dakota, occurs in the last major battle between United States troops and Native Americans, and hundreds of Native American men, women, and children are slain, along with 29 soldiers

1892
- Ellis Island in New York becomes the immigration center in America

1893
- U.S. Marines interfere in the Kingdom of Hawaii, which leads to the overthrow of Queen Liliuokalani
- New York Stock Exchange collapses
- Chicago World Columbian Exposition

1894
- The first public showing of Thomas Edison's kinetoscope motion picture

1895
- The first United States patent for the automobile is granted to George B. Selden for his two-stroke automobile engine

1896
- Republican William McKinley becomes president
- George Washington Carver was appointed director of agricultural research at Tuskegee Institute

1897
- The first Boston Marathon

1898
- Battleship USS Main is sunk in Havana Harbor
- Blockade of Cuba begins
- San Juan, Puerto Rico, is bombed during the Spanish-American Wars, and Spain later ceded Puerto Rico, Guam, and the Philippines to the U.S.

1899
- Philippines begin to fight back to regain their independence from America
- U.S. creates an open-door policy with China

1900
- President William McKinley wins his second term

1901
- Only six months into his term, President William H.McKinley is shot at the Pan American Exposition in Buffalo, New York; he later dies
- Vice President Theodore Roosevelt is inaugurated as president upon the death of William McKinley

---

1902 – 1922

Presidents

Theodore Roosevelt, William Howard Taft, Woodrow Wilson, Warren G. Harding.

This period in history is normally referred to as the progressive era to the new era. This is also a time when businesses and government worked to make the country a safer place in which to live and work. This was also a time for our nation to become a more democratic society, (not to be confused as Democratic Party) with the right of women to vote expanded, direct election of senators, and a number of election reforms. America entered World War I to help make the global world a safer place in which to live. America took flight and to the roads, and to the airways with radio. America begins to roar into the '20s, "The Roaring Twenties" as it is historically referred to.

Events

1903
- Harley-Davidson motorcycle company created

- Ford Motor Company created
- First World Series in baseball
- Department of Commerce and Labor created
- Wright brothers make their first powered flight

1904
- U.S. establishes international policing power regarding Latin American countries
- World's Fair St. Louis

1905
- Theodore Roosevelt begins full term as President

1906
- San Francisco earthquake

1908
- Ford Model T car is now for sale
- William Howard Taft elected President

1909
- U.S. penny design changed from an Indian head to a Lincoln head
- NAACP founded
- Tariff Act created

1911
- Supreme Court breaks up Standard Oil

1912
- Theodore Roosevelt shot but not killed
- Woodrow Wilson elected President

1913
- Woman Suffrage demonstration in Washington, D.C.
- 16th Amendment, establishing income tax
- 17th Amendment, establishing direct election of U.S. Senators

1914
- Mother's Day established as a national holiday
- Federal Trade Commission created

1915
- RMS Lusitania sunk

1916
- Jeannette Rankin first woman elected to U.S. Congress
- Woodrow Wilson is reelected President

1917
- U.S. enters World War I

1918
- Armistice agreement ends World War I
- Spanish flu pandemic begins

1919
- 18th Amendment, establishing Prohibition

1920
- 19th Amendment grants women the right to vote
- First radio broadcasts by KDKA in Pittsburgh, and WWJ in Detroit

1921
- Religious services first broadcast on the radio
- First air mail plane took flight from California to New York
- Warren G. Harding becomes 29th President
- First microfilm device introduced

1922
- Warren Harding is first President heard on radio
- All homes required to have mailboxes
- Greek Orthodox Archdiocese was established in the U.S.

1923 – 1943

Presidents

Warren G. Harding, Calvin Coolidge, Herbert Hoover, Franklin D. Roosevelt

These next 20 years saw yet again many technological and social advancements, as well as declines in race relationships with African Americans. But there were those who prevailed and moved equality forward. There was also the Great Depression, which affected the lives and livelihoods of millions of Americans. On a positive note, President Hoover created the public works project to put many Americans into new jobs. Radio and television began to expand channels of national communication, with Americans sharing the news and entertainment. The Social Security Act was created, providing some retirement income for future wage earners. Unfortunately, these 20 years saw the devastating World War II lead us into the beginning of the next 20 years of our history.

Events

1923
- President Harding dies suddenly
- Vice President Calvin Coolidge becomes President

1924
- Spelman Seminary becomes Spelman College

1925
- Coolidge's second inauguration

- American Negro Labor Congress founded
- Scopes monkey trial: Biology teacher tried for teaching evolution

1926
- Historian Carter G. Woodson proposes Negro History Week

1927
- Charles Lindberg nonstop transatlantic flight
- Philo Farnsworth demonstrates the first television

1929
- Herbert Hoover inaugurated as 31st President
- Clarence Birdseye offers his quick-frozen food to the public

1930
- Great Depression

1931
- "Star-Spangled Banner" is adopted as the national anthem

1932
- First woman elected to the U.S. Senate, Hattie W. Caraway

1933
- Franklin D. Roosevelt is inaugurated as the 32nd President
- Prohibition is repealed

1935
- Social Security Act passed

1936
- American sprinter Jesse Owens wins four gold medals at the 1936 Summer Olympics in Berlin
- Bureau of Investigation becomes the FBI under J. EdgarHoover

1937
- Franklin Roosevelt's second inauguration

1939
- New York World's Fair
- World War II starts in Europe; U.S. is neutral
- Franklin Roosevelt's third inauguration; the first and only president elected to a third term
- John Atanasoff and Clifford Berry of Iowa State College complete the prototype of the first digital computer

1940
- Invention of the Jeep

1941
- Japan attacks Hawaii at Pearl Harbor
- U.S. declares war on Japan
- U.S. enters World War II
- U.S. Army forms African American air combat units, the Tuskegee Airmen

1942
- University of Chicago produces the first controlled, self-sustaining nuclear chain reaction

1944 – 1964

Presidents
Harry S. Truman, Dwight D. Eisenhower, John F. Kennedy.

It seems that every 20 years America is in a war or other civil conflicts. Even as we are advancing with technologies that are changing our ways of life and communication, we are still learning how to be civil with one another. America elects as President a young inspirational leader, John F. Kennedy, who said, "Ask not what your country can do for you, but what you can do for your country," only to later be assassinated.

Events
1944
- June 6, 1944 - The Normandy Invasion, D-Day

1945
- Franklin Roosevelt's fourth inauguration
- President Roosevelt dies of a stroke and is succeeded by his Vice President, Harry Truman
- President Truman authorizes the dropping of two atomic bombs on Japan
- United Nations established in New York City

1946
- The island nation of the Philippines is granted independence by the United States
- The computer age begins as the Electronic Numerical Integrator and Computer (ENIAC), the first vacuum-tube computer, is built for the U.S. military
- National School Lunch Act approved by Congress

1947
- Central Intelligence Agency is established

1948
- Congress passes foreign aid bill

1949
- Truman's second inauguration

- Captain James Gallagher achieves first around-the-world nonstop airplane flight

1950
- U.S. enters the Korean War

1951
- The inauguration of transcontinental television occurs with the broadcast of President Truman's speech at the Japanese Peace Treaty Conference in San Francisco
- Richard Buckminster Fuller files patent for the Geodesic Dome

1952
- General Dwight D. Eisenhower elected as president

1953
- Korean War ends
- First color television goes on sale

1954
- Large-scale polio vaccination initiated
- Racial segregation in public schools is declared unconstitutional by the U.S. Supreme Court

1955
- The U.S. government agrees to train South Vietnamese troops
- Disneyland opens in Anaheim, California
- The first transatlantic telephone cable begins operation
- Interstate highway system begins with the signing of theFederal-Aid Highway Act
- Rosa Parks, a seamstress from Montgomery, Alabama, refuses to give up her seat on the bus to a Caucasian passenger and is subsequently arrested and fined. A year later, in the case of Browder v.

Gale, the U.S. Supreme Court rules that segregated seating on buses is unconstitutional

1957
- President Eisenhower elected to a second term
- U.S. Congress approves the first civil rights bill since reconstruction with additional protection of voting rights

1958
- Explorer I, the first U.S. space satellite

1959
- Alaska and Hawaii become the 49th and 50th state to the United States
- NASA selects the first seven military pilots to become the Mercury Seven, the first astronauts of the United States; the Mercury Seven were John Glenn, Scott Carpenter, Gordon Cooper, Gus Grissom, Wally Schirra, Alan Shepard, and Deke Slayton

1960
- Four African American college students from North Carolina Agricultural and Technical College in Greensboro, North Carolina, stage a sit-in at a segregated Woolworth lunch counter, protesting their denial of service
- The 50-star flag of the United States is debuted in Philadelphia
- John F. Kennedy elected President

1961
- The first U.S. manned suborbital space flight is completed, followed later by John Glenn orbits of the earth in 1962
- President Kennedy announces his intention to place

a man on the moon by the end of the decade

1962

- The Cuban Missile Crises begins
- Three thousand troops quell riots, allowing James Meredith to enter the University of Mississippi as the first African American student under guard by federal marshals

1963

- The Supreme Court of the United States ruled in the case of Abington School District vs. Schempp that laws requiring the recitation of the Lord's Prayer or Bible verses in public schools is unconstitutional
- The Civil Rights march on Washington, D.C., for jobs and freedom culminates with Dr. Martin Luther King Jr.'s famous "I Have a Dream" speech from the steps of the Lincoln Memorial
- President John F. Kennedy is mortally wounded by assassin, Lee Harvey Oswald
- Vice President Lyndon B. Johnson is sworn into office

1964

- U.S. Congress passes an omnibus legislation on Civil Rights.
- It banned discrimination in jobs, voting and accommodations
- President Lyndon B. Johnson wins his first presidential election
- The Civil Rights Act becomes law

Presidents

Lyndon B. Johnson, Richard Nixon, Gerald Ford, Jimmy Carter, Ronald Reagan.

An amazing 20 years in American history! The best part is that I and many readers of this book were affected and amazed with events that took place, and for each of us these experiences are varied. I remember listening to Martin Luther King Jr. speak on his "I have a dream" vision. Watching men land and walk on the moon. The gasoline crisis in the '70s, not knowing if you would be able to purchase gasoline on any given day. Buying our first house when mortgage rates were as high as 14%. The insertion of new computer technologies by IBM and Apple. The draft, life lost by our military, and the protests. The election of a movie star and governor as President of the United States. As we continue the timeline, younger generations that read this book will begin to recall events and actions that impacted their lives.

Events

1965

- Martin Luther King speaks at a civil rights rally on the courthouse steps of the Alabama State Capitol, ending the Selma to Montgomery, Alabama, march for voting rights

- The Voting Rights Act of 1965 is signed into law by President Lyndon B. Johnson

1966
- America is in the Vietnam war
- United States warplanes begin their bombing raids of Hanoi and Haiphong, North Vietnam
- Medicare, the government medical program for citizens over the age of 65, begins
- The first African American United States Senator in eighty-five years, Edward Brooke, is elected to Congress

1967
- Race riots plague U.S. cities. In Newark, New Jersey, 26 are killed, 500 injured and 1,000 arrested from July 12 to 17; One week later, July 23 to 30, 40 killed, 2,000 injured, and 5,000 left homeless after rioting in Detroit, known as the 12th Street Riots, decimate an African American ghetto: riots eventually stopped by over 12,500 Federal troopers and National Guardsmen
- Thurgood Marshall is sworn into office as the first African American Supreme Court Justice

1968
- Civil Rights leader Martin Luther King Jr. is assassinated in Memphis, Tennessee, while standing on a motel balcony, by James Earl Ray
- Richard M. Nixon re-elected as President
- McCarver Elementary School in Tacoma, Washington, becomes the nation's first magnet school

1969

- Four-party Vietnam War peace talks begin. America withdraws from the Vietnam War
- United States puts Neil Armstrong and Edwin E. Aldrin Jr. on the surface of the moon
- The Internet, called Arpanet during its initial development, is invented
- U.S. Supreme Court rules that students' First Amendment rights were violated when they were suspended for wearing black arm bands to protest the Vietnam War

1970

- First Earth Day celebration
- First Mexican American Catholic bishop
- The gas shortage of the 1970s

1972

- The Watergate crisis begins
- President Nixon reelected
- Texas Instruments introduces the first in its line of electronic hand-held calculators

1973

- The United States Supreme Court rules in Roe vs. Wade that a woman cannot be prevented by a state from having an abortion during the first six months of pregnancy
- Vice President Spiro T. Agnew resigns amid charges of tax evasion and is replaced by the appointment of Gerald R. Ford
- The Arab Oil Embargo creates the 1973 energy crisis

1974
- Impeachment hearings are begun by the House Judiciary Committee against President Richard M. Nixon
- President Richard M. Nixon resigns the office of the presidency, avoiding the impeachment process and admitting his role in the Watergate affair; V.P. Gerald Ford becomes President

1976
- The Viking 1 space probe successfully lands on Mars
- Jimmy Carter elected president

1977
- The movie "Star Wars" opens and becomes the highest grossing film at the time
- The cabinet level Energy Department is created by President Jimmy Carter
- Apple Computer, now Apple Inc., introduces the Apple II, one of the first successful personal computers

1978
- The Camp David Peace Agreement between Israel and Egypt is formulated

1979
- Accident at the Three Mile Island nuclear power plant in Middletown, Pennsylvania; Worst in the world until Chernobyl

1980
- Winter Olympic Games are held in in the United States

- The United States Olympic Committee withdraws its athletes from participation in the Moscow Summer Olympic Games due to the continued involvement of the Soviet Union in Afghanistan
- The Mount St. Helens volcano, in Washington State, erupts
- Ronald Reagan elected president, beating Jimmy Carter

1981
- President Ronald Reagan survives an assignation attempt
- IBM introduces the IBM-PC personal computer

1982
- The Senate passes a bill that virtually eliminates the practice of bussing to achieve racial integration
- The Knoxville World's Fair opens
- The Vietnam Veterans Memorial is dedicated
- The highest unemployment rate since 1940 is recorded

1983
- Astronaut Sally Ride becomes the first American woman to travel into space

1984
- First U.S. space walk by Navy Captain Bruce McCandless and Army Lt. Colonel Robert Stewart
- The opening ceremony of the Los Angeles Olympic Games is held
- President Ronald Reagan wins a landslide reelection

1985

- The first meeting in six years between the leaders of the Soviet Union and the United States occurs when Mikhail Gorbachev and Ronald Reagan engage in a five-hour summit conference in Geneva, Switzerland
- The first version of the Windows operating system for computers is released
- U.S. Supreme Court finds that Alabama statutes authorizing silent prayer and teacher-led voluntary prayer in public schools violate the First Amendment

---

1986 – 2006

Presidents
Ronald Reagan, George H. W. Bush, Bill Clinton.

The Reagan revolution continues. His words to tear down the wall in Berlin eventually lead to it actually happening, and then later the reunification of East and West occurs. Those achievements get quickly overshadowed by the terrorist events soon to come, both during the Clinton presidency and later the attacks on the World Trade Center and the Pentagon, with one jet being taken down by brave Americans on board. America now continues to recover and revive from those terrible events. Life goes on. Technology expands our computer and communication usages.

Events

1986

- Martin Luther King Day is officially observed for the first time as a federal holiday in the United States
- The stock market crash known as Black Monday

1987

- Famous "Tear down that wall" speech by President Ronald Ragan

1989

- Vice President under Ronald Reagan, George Herbert Walker Bush, claims victory in the presidential election over Democratic challenger Michael S. Dukakis
- University of Phoenix establishes their "online campus," the first to offer online bachelor's and master's degrees
- WORLD WIDE WEB: Invented by Tim Berners-Lee, it would soon change the way governments, businesses, and people operate

1990

- The Hubble Telescope is placed into orbit by the United States Space Shuttle Discovery
- U.S. President George H.W. Bush and his Soviet counterpart Mikhail Gorbachev sign a treaty to eliminate chemical weapons production
- Americans with Disabilities Act (ADA) becomes law
- Douglas Wilder becomes the first elected African American governor as he takes office in Richmond, Virginia

1991
- U.S. Congress passes a resolution authorizing the use of force to liberate Kuwait

1992
- Bill Clinton elected President of the United States

1993
- The World Trade Center is bombed by Islamic terrorists when a van parked below the North Tower explodes
- Intel ships the first Pentium chips, revolutionizing the processing of computers around the world
- The North American Free Trade Agreement (NAFTA) goes into effect
- President Bill Clinton signs the Assault Weapons Ban, which bars the use of these weapons for 10 years
- E-MAIL: Electronic mail goes back to the 1960s, but it really started taking off with Web use. By 1997, the volume of business e-mail surpassed that of regular mail

1994
- The Republican revolution is strong with the midterm elections when, for the first time in 40 years, the party gains control of both the Senate and the U.S. House of Representatives
- Whiteboards find their way into U.S. classrooms in increasing numbers and begin to replace blackboards

1995

- Anarchists Timothy McVeigh and Terry Nichols explode a bomb outside the Murrah Federal Building in Oklahoma City, killing 168 people in a domestic terrorism attack

1996

- The Summer Olympic Games are opened in Atlanta, Georgia, by President Bill Clinton
- Centennial Park bombing of Olympic tourists
- President Clinton wins a second term

1998

- The Monica Lewinsky scandal begins when U.S. President Bill Clinton denies his relationship with the White House intern in a televised interview; this denial, and other denials to a grand jury investigation, would lead to the impeachment of the president

1999

- President Bill Clinton is acquitted by the U.S. Senate in the Monica Lewinsky scandal
- Two Columbine High School students go on a killing spree that leaves 15 dead and 23 wounded at the Littleton, Colorado school

2000

- George W. Bush elected as President (the son of President George H. W. Bush)
- Bush also establishes the White House Office of Faith-Based and Community Initiatives
- The controversial No Child Left Behind Act (NCLB) is approved by Congress and signed into law by President Bush

- Hillary Rodham Clinton wins a seat for the United States Senate from New York. It is the first time a former First Lady wins public office

2001

- Tiger Woods becomes the first golfer to hold all four major titles simultaneously
- Islamic fundamentalist terrorists hijack four U.S. airliners and crash them into the Pentagon in Arlington, Virginia, and the World Trade Center in New York City; the fourth plane is heroically crashedby passengers into a Shanksville, Pennsylvania cornfield
- In response to the tragedy of September 11, the United States military, with participation from ally United Kingdom, commence the first attack in the War on Terrorism on the Taliban and Al-Qaeda in Afghanistan, by November 12, the Taliban government leaves the capital, Kabul

2002

- Winter Olympic Games are opened by President George W. Bush in Salt Lake City, Utah

2003

- A tragedy at NASA occurs when the Space Shuttle Columbia explodes upon reentry over Texas, all seven astronauts are killed
- The U.S. coalition seizes control of Baghdad in the Iraq conflict
- Saddam Hussein, former leader of Iraq, is captured in a small bunker in Tikrit by the U.S. 4th Infantry Division
- The groundbreaking ceremony for the Freedom Tower at Ground Zero

2004
- President George W. Bush wins reelection over Democratic Senator John Kerry
- Hurricane Katrina strikes the Gulf Coast

2006
- In the midterm elections, both houses of Congress change back to Democratic hands for the first time since 1994

2007 – Present

Presidents
George W. Bush, Barack H. Obama, Donald J. Trump

Events

2007
- The first female speaker of the U.S. House of Representatives, Representative Nancy Pelosi of San Francisco, California
- President George W. Bush announces a troop surge of 21,500 for the war in Iraq

2008
- Emergency Economic Stabilization Act

2009
- Barack Obama takes the oath of office for President of the United States, becoming the nation's first African American President
- Tea Party protests spring up across the nation
- The H1N1 virus, named the Swine Flu, is deemed a global pandemic

- An economic recession deepens as jobless claims climb above 10%
- President Obama announces a surge of 30,000 additional troops to Afghanistan to stem increased efforts by the Taliban in the country
- The U.S. House of Representatives finalizes the health care legislation approved by the Senate, extending health benefits and insurance to most Americans, and the legislation of the Affordable Care Act passes, passed on a partisan basis by the Democratic majority

2010

- Biggest turnaround in congressional seats since 1948, and many attribute the election to disfavor of Obama administration spending practices, including the health care legislation passed in March

2011

- Osama Bin Laden, mastermind of the 9/11, 2001 attacks on the World Trade Center, the Pentagon, and other locations and leader of the terrorist group, Al-Qaeda, is killed after 10 years of pursuit by United States
- The final shuttle flight lands at the Kennedy Space Center, signifying the end of the NASA shuttle space program
- The war in Iraq is declared over when President Obama orders the last combat troops to leave the country

2012

- The first licenses for cars without drivers is granted in the state of Nevada to Google; futuristic transportation systems

- President Barack Obama wins a significant victory, 332 electoral votes to 206, for his second term in office

2013

- Using a 3-D printer and cell cultures, American scientists at Cornell University grow a living ear
- Two bombs explode near the finish line of the Boston Marathon, killing three and injuring hundreds in a terrorist attack coordinated by two brothers associated with radical Islam
- The Affordable Care Act, called Obamacare, begins registering people for the expanded federal government health insurance program despite a variety of waivers and problems in implementing the cumbersome rules and regulations

2014

- First case of Ebola is certified in the United States, an outcome of travel from Liberia and West Africa where the virus has spread to 22,000 people and killed 9,000

2015

- Full diplomatic relations are reestablished between the United States and Cuba for the first time in 54 years

2016

- Terrorist attack in Orlando, Florida, with 50 killed and 53 wounded, considered inspired by ISIS and radical Islamic terrorists
- Donald J. Trump elected as president

2017

- SpaceX, the private aeronautic firm, engages in first reflight of an orbital class rocket, which can land vertically on a platform
- North Korea fires ballistic missile over the Sea of Japan, testing the resolve of the world
- United States withdraws from the Paris Climate Agreement
- President Trump signs the largest tax cut and changes in the tax code since 1986

2018

- Meetings between the President Donald Trump and North Korean Leader Kim Jong-un become the first summit between leaders of the two nations, with discussions about North Korea giving up its ambitions for nuclear weapons
- Tariffs against $34 billion of Chinese goods go into effect
- Midterm elections result in Democratic gains of 40 seats in the U.S. House of Representatives
- Partial government shutdown begins after President Trump refuses to sign any spending package for Homeland Security that does not include border barrier funding in appropriations due to the status of illegal immigration and border security; shutdown lasts for 35 days, the longest shutdown in U.S. history

2019

- Tiger Woods wins his 15th Major at the Masters
- Stock market closes above 28,000 in the Dow Jones Average for the first time, continuing its rise, with 22 record closes through the year

- President Donald Trump is impeached by the House of Representatives in a partisan vote
- USMCA (United States, Mexico, Canada Agreement) trade deal passed by the House of Representatives, replacing NAFTA with agreement with fairer provisions for the United States between the North American nations of Canada, Mexico
- President Trump approved Keystone Xl and Dakota Access Pipelines
- President Trump nominates Neil Gorsuch for the U.S. Supreme Court
- President Trump creates the Office of American Innovation
- President Trump donates his first-quarter salary to the National Park Service
- U.S. repairs and builds new border walls
- President Trump signed the historic FIRST STEP Act into law

2020

- President orders a strike that killed the No. 1 terrorist in the world, Qasem Soleimani.
- Seven million people exited the food stamp program
- Unemployment rate is at a record low, at or below 4%
- China pandemic outbreak in the U.S. (COVID-19)
- USMCA trade deal completed
- Defense Production act by the president to increase production of necessary products to counter COVID-19
- Presidential executive order to reduce cost of drugs to Americans

•Election year and Donald J. Trump is selected for a second term as presidential candidate by the Republican Party and Joe Biden selected as the Democratic Party presidential candidate

For the remaining years to complete this twenty-year segment your must fill in the blanks. We have a presidential election still being challenged. We are still in a Covid Crisis. What will be our history in the next seven years? What will you write? Please let you children know about these seven years from your history.

2021
•
•

2022
•
•

2023
•
•

2024
•
•

2025
•
•

2026
•
•

2027
•
•

Learn from the past but
Teach and Lead for the Future

Welcome now to 2020! You have now taken a journey of 244 years of American history since this country became the United States of America officially in 1776. Yes, there is much in our history before 1776, but this timeline begins when we are officially the United States. Let me remind you that I am not a historian but an average American citizen much like you, the reader. Our important history seems to get edited more and more to convey a specific message or to ignore a specific message and incident. As I researched events for this timeline, I have tried to include what has stood out to me as important historical happenings including those of patriots, politicians, women, African Americans, Native Americans, religious moments, times of hardship and success, times of innovation and discovery.

This timeline can serve you as a launching pad to share our history with your children.. As you observe and share with your children significant turning points and helping points of what those before us have done, you might say, well, the author did not mention this or that in his timeline. I say to you, congratulations on your knowledge of American history! Write it down in this book to make it more personal, and I challenge you to help others remember our great American historical heritage.

As this paragraph is being written on this day 9/2/2020, I look around, and this world, as well as this nation, is going through unbelievable adjustments in our health, our homes, our politics, and our commerce, our education, our beliefs. This book began with July 4th, and we must learn from the past to teach and lead for the future as we move forward to make America even greater again. So, as you have discovered by now, we are on a journey to **"Never Stop Teaching and Leading, Keep America Great."** Where does that teaching begin, but in the home. So, journey with me to Chapter 2, where we can learn what to do in the home that builds a strong foundation for our children to have the courage, strength, knowledge, and faith to be proud, productive Americans who will preserve what the founding of this great nation was about.

CHAPTER TWO

Teaching and Leading in Your Home

Welcome home! Just stop and think for a moment where your first teaching and leading took place? I do not believe that anyone could not say that it did not start in the home with family. Well, home and family can mean a lot of things to many people.

If you are leading from the home, you might be in one many Family types. Melissa Mayntz provides a good definition of Family, and I quote her:

Basic Family Definition

"In the most basic definition, a group of people who share a legal bond or a blood bond is a family.
- **Legal Bonds**: Families are legally bound through marriages, adoptions, and guardianships, including the rights, duties, and obligations of those legal contracts. Legal bonds can be changed, expanded, or dissolved to change the composition of a family.
- **Blood Bonds**: Individuals who are directly related through a common ancestor are part of a family. This includes both close and distant relatives such as siblings, parents, grandparents, aunts, uncles, nieces, nephews, and cousins. Researching a family tree or genealogical records can reveal familial blood bonds.

Despite the apparent simplicity of this definition of family, the idea of family goes far beyond just legal or blood relationships for many people.
Types of Families
There are different types of family structures, each of which is equally viable as a supportive, caring unit.
- **Nuclear Family**: Also called a conjugal family, a nuclear family includes the parents and their children living in the same residence or sharing the closest bonds.
- **Extended Family**: This type of family includes all relatives in close proximity, such as grandparents, aunts, uncles, and cousins. In a

family household that is extended, these relatives typically live together and all share daily household duties. This type of family is also called a joint family or multigenerational family, depending on which members are included.

•**Complex Family**: This type of extended family has three or more adults, plus their children. This type of family may be formed through divorce and remarriage, or it may be formed through polygamy in societies where that practice is acceptable. Some families may be complex even without formal legal bonds between the adults.

•**Single Parent Family**: This family type includes one parent and their children only. A single parent family could be the result of a divorce, the death of one parent, or even a single parent adoption.

•**Stepfamily**: This is a family where the adults have divorced and remarried, bringing children from other unions together to form a new nuclear family. The children may come from several different parents or be on one or both sides of the new union. Stepfamilies are also referred to as blended families because they are a blend of two or more different families.

•**Traditional Family**: This is a family unit defined in the classic sense as the father working outside the home to support the members financially, while the mother remains at home and tends to domestic duties and child-rearing. This strict definition of family is less and less common in modern society.

•**Adopted Family**: This type of family shares

legal bonds but not genetic ones. Two parents may adopt a child to whom they share no blood relationship, or one parent may adopt the child of the other parent. Adopted families can also be defined in an emotional or spiritual sense where no formal legal bonds are present.

•**Foster Family**: A foster family includes one or more adult parent who serves as a temporary guardian for one or more children to whom they may or may not be biologically related. In time, more formal arrangements may be made, and foster children can be legally adopted.

•**Childless Family**: This type of family includes a couple with no children. Couples may choose not to have children or may be prevented from having children biologically due to medical reasons. Some childless families might include pets viewed as family members.

I believe that most of us would connect with one or more of these defined family types. As for me growing up, I lived mostly in an extended family, starting out in the traditional family, then in the first grade living with my aunt and uncle and their children, then living with my mother and grandparents. This is the environment where my life was enriched by adults teaching and leading me until I graduated from high school. That in itself is an amazing story, and if you want to learn more about that story, it is told in another book of mine: "Never Stop! Asking, discovering, and sharing!"

OK. Now let us start with the traditional family. What techniques are available for parents to teach and lead their children? Obviously, for infants the family should begin as a team. Even though the mother may have given birth, or not, the value of both parents' involvement in the early years of development is immeasurable. They should be a team and share responsibilities if possible, like: diapers, feeding, rocker time, walking time, and talking time.

As the infant progresses to the talking and walking stages, parents' daily life structure becomes more real and noticeable to the child.

Children

As your children grow its important for them to know their relationship in the family and the expectations that you as parents have for them. This verse acts as a a powerful biblical guideline.

Proverbs 22:6 ESV
Train up a child in the way he should go; even when he is old, he will not depart from it.

But we must go beyond just the words of this verse, we must put into practice those things that will make our children honorable, responsible, and patriotic Americans with a strong faith in what they believe.

What are some of the first responsibilities for our children as we are teaching and leading them? Teaching them to take care of themselves is unbelievably important as one day they will actually have to take care of themselves. What do some of those responsibilities and actions and traits include for our children?

•**Honesty**: Your children must be taught the value of always being truthful, and as the expression goes, "Be truthful even if it hurts."

I have told my children if you lose everything, even the clothes on your back, the one thing you still have left of value is your honesty and integrity.

•**Sharing**: Sharing really becomes difficult, especially at an early age. It may not always be possible to share, something but be parental leaders that they might see what sharing is by your actions. Teach them to always share, if possible.

•**Kindness**: It is amazing sometimes when we see a toddler hug another toddler. It's out of unrestrained emotions. Oh! If those acts of kindness would carry through their lives! But remember that our children are always silently looking at us and observing us. As parents we must also be kind by examples, sharing examples and honest examples as well.

Other ways that we can teach and lead our children is through discipline. I do not know about you, but as for me this is one of the most challenging things that I have to do for myself, much less teach and lead my children. So, what are some of the early things we as parents can do to establish discipline and instill the importance of a routine in one's life at an early age. Here are some responsibilities that can occur on a regular basis:

•Make your bed: When a child is old enough, they should be taught how to make their own bed. US Admiral William H. McCraven had this to say about making your bed in the morning:

"If you make your bed every morning, you will have accomplished the first task of the day. It will give you a small sense of pride, and it will encourage you to do another task, and another, and another. And by the end of the day that one task completed will have turned into many tasks completed."

- **Take care of yourself**: This is an overly broad subject area and can include many things and should be taught when children are able to achieve these skills on their own. The basics must include skills about basic hygiene: brushing your teeth, bathing, etc. Remember that one day your children will have to take care of themselves. How you lead them now will affect their lives in the future.
- **Keep a schedule**: Looking back, I now can reflect on how important this is. It's not like living by the clock, but rather developing a family living routine. During the school year it is getting ready for breakfast, getting ready for school, returning home from school or afternoon activities, returning home, getting time for family, homework, play, or personal time. Keeping a schedule gives order and direction in one's life. Now that is not to say that a schedule cannot be broken, which I guarantee will happen at some time.
- **Responsibilities**: Children should have responsibilities as they grow and mature. Those responsibilities can evolve from one task to many, which could include some of the following depending on their age and their abilities. These responsibilities could take on two forms.

1. **Tasks**: Some might call these chores that assign responsibility to various children in the household. I did an Excel web search for a weekly chore spreadsheet, and one that I found is illustrated below. I am only showing a part of this full-week schedule. Of course, you can make your own, but I wanted to share this with the readers to stimulate some thought about tasks.

Weekly Chore Schedule

Task	Sun 8/30/2020		Mon 8/31/2020		Tue 9/1/2020	
	Who	Done	Who	Done	Who	Done
Pick Up Toys/Misc	Terry	✓ Done				
Get Mail	David	✓ Done				
Take Out Trash	John					
Dinner Dishes						
Dust						
Sweep						
Vacuum						

2. **Tasks with rewards**: At some point in a child's life it's important to learn the value of rewards from work. So, the parents might decide to incentify chores. Develop in your children a sense of working for pay. After all, that is what they will be doing one day as Americans. Teach and lead them on how to earn and save, so that they might make

sound decisions with your guidance on how to spend their money. I must share this story about one of my grandchildren, who at the age of 13 for his birthday, requested money as a gift so that he might invest it in the stock market! Wow! At age 13! Absolutely amazing! If you are looking for a place to start, illustrated below is an example of another Excel spreadsheet you can download from the internet to track earned tasks.

Robin's Allowance Tracker

Tasks	Value	SUN	MON	TUE	WED	THU	FRI	SAT	Total
Make bed	$0.50	✓	✓		✓				$1.50
Pickup toys	$0.50		✓	✓					$1.00
Clean room	$0.50								
Clean dining table	$1.00			✓					$1.00
Sweep floor	$1.00								
Feed pet	$1.00	✓	✓	✓	✓				$4.00
Water plants	$1.00								
Date allowance given:	5/5/2020					Total allowance earned:			$7.50

As we consider these previous suggestions that begin to form a foundation of expectations for our children, we can also draw reference from the Bible as well.

Colossians 3:20 ESV
Children, obey your parents in everything, for this pleases the Lord.

Proverbs 6:20 ESV
My son, keep your father's commandment, and forsake not your mother's teaching.

Galatians 5:22-23 ESV
But the fruit of the Spirit is love, joy, peace, patience, kindness, goodness, faithfulness, gentleness, self-control; against such things there is no law.

As this verse implies, the fruit of the Spirit is encouragement for our children and guides parents as to how they should lead, especially in these times of 2020. During this elections year, we do see results of Galatians 5:22-23. Just look at the health care professionals, fire fighters, and those good police officers who are helping where possible. There are many others to mention, as well. Do not forget the church and the Christian volunteers that are helping in the community, as well as other nonprofit organizations.

But let us not forget what is also happening in 2020. Riots are generated by groups like ANTIFA. Look at all of the murders and thefts taking place. It saddens me to know that these adults have been led astray by someone or some group, or they have lost their faith or never found it. I wonder if they even consider what their parents might think of their actions and the harm they are causing to others? How do we as parents establish a strong foundation for our children before they leave us so as not to stray from God's will? The next section of this chapter will provide some guidance that we as parents can do as teachers and leaders of our children.

What an awesome responsibility to be a parent! Just think about the young parents in 1776 when our nation was founded. There were no educational institutions except in large cities, no computers, television, phones, etc. All schooling was home schooling or in groups. There was almost no such thing as a professional teacher. In 1776 there were no public libraries. Students wrote on slate boards, as there were no pencils or paper. Many students just learned how to read and do math. Education at this time was mostly for white males. Some women received higher education, but very few. Everyone else was excluded. The role of parents was made even more instrumental because they were the educators, as they became teachers and leaders in their familes.

In today's time, many parents are doing just that, home schooling their children for various reasons in 2020. It could be the COVID-19 pandemic, it could be that parents do not like the pedagogy of public schools and the slant in education that is drawing our children further away from Americanism. So, what are some of the important values parents have to give to their children?

Be available: Being a parent is a 24-hour-a-day responsibility. You know what I mean. When your baby wakes up early in the morning and needs your attention and loving care, you are there to comfort and care for them. Care never stops, even when they become adults. They are still your children, and you want to be available when you can.

Be calm: Especially in a crisis. Your emotions can, as

the expression goes, "fuel the flames." Have I always been calm in a crisis? The answer is no. But I try very hard to remain calm, as I can see that it seems to calm others around me so that wise decisions can be made as all move forward from crisis to calm.

Be loving: As parents we pray that our children are able to recognize our love for them. Sharing is an extremely important part of loving. Your children must see through your actions, your words, and your love for them. Here are some things you can do:
- •Tell them you love them
- •Give praise when due
- •Spend more time together in quality activities
- •Give them your undivided attention one on one
- •Talk to them, not at them or down to them

Be serious and consistent: Our children in their early years need to learn when a parent is serious. This only happens if we develop a consistent nature about ourselves as parents so that our children can see the serious and not-so-serious side of our leadership in the home. So when we say No! they understand that's the end of the discussion, unless they are able to convince a parent to reconsider. That takes us back to the loving attribute we need. So, what you are reading into this is that parenting is not as simple as comparing apples to oranges.

Be helpful: Does this ever ring truer than in 2020? Our children are exposed to an unbelievable amount of information and stress in these times. Now, more than in my time growing up, balance in one's schedule is uniquely different. Teach them the importance of a schedule and being on time. Refer back to my bullet point on "Keep a schedule." A part of being helpful is also being motivational to our children. Encourage them to set goals and make decisions. Encourage them to be the best in whatever they do, whether it's academics, athletics, music, etc.

Being helpful also requires that you teach them how to deal with failure. I cannot begin to tell you how important this is, and not to dwell on failure too long. Our children must realize that it's going to happen to all of us at one time or another, and that failure can be one of the most important learning moments in our lives. In my previous book, "Never Stop! Asking, discovering, and sharing!", you can find stories from many people about failures and discoveries and how they have been life changing. The point here is that we must learn from failure and help our children set a path to success.

As parents, there are many other things we should teach and expose our children to so that one day we pray that they will take the lessons learned from us and apply them to their families.

Teach decision-making skills: We are not with our children all of the time, and they must be taught how to make decisions on their own and learn the importance of being able to say No! to something that could harm them, could cause them to be immoral,or could harm another.

What a shame. Just look at the news in 2020 and the harm that is being caused by others because of a change in their decision-making skills. Where in their lives did they decide to kill another, burn a building down, or disrespect the values of our nation? Do their parents know? Were they taught to be Americans who respect our country? Let's not fail the next generation as we continue to teach our children to Keep America Great. Perhaps we need to apply some of the following teaching and leadership skills to our young.

Teach them to pray: I still remember as a young boy the first prayer taught to me. My mother would kneel beside me at my bed and taught me the following prayer:

> "Now I lay me down to sleep,
> I pray the Lord my Soul to keep.
> If I should die before I 'wake,
> I pray the Lord my Soul to take."

Hanging above my bed was this print of the Good Shepherd, which hangs in my house today.

The inscription at the bottom of the engraving reads:

"I am the Good Shepherd, and know my sheep, and know of mine, and I lay down my life for the sheep."

As parents, I pray that we would do the same for our children in America. We love our children, and we would lay down our lives for them. From conception on.

Take them to Church: As we reflect back on our history and the founding of our great nation, at the cornerstone of that foundation is our faith. Our country was founded on Judeo-Christian belief. Churches in America were established before government was created. In church our children will continue to learn about love and forgiveness and how to apply it. As parents in the home we should also be loving and forgiving to our children. We must also teach our children to be loving and forgiving to others. It is a hard thing to do at first, but when you forgive someone, it sets you free. You might not forget, but you will have taken the higher road and become stronger within yourself. You may impact another person in a positive way that might change their future actions.

In church your children will be with others their own age, as they are taught together what it means to be a Christian. One day they may have the opportunity to lead others in faith because of the action you took as a parent by taking them to church. Do you remember those times in church with your family? Take time and share those memories with your children.

This simple act among Americans must increase and not decrease. Our churches must not decrease in numbers but increase in numbers. We must teach and lead our children as Christians.

1 John 3:18 ESV
Little children, let us not love in word or talk but in deed and in truth.

Teach life and learning skills: Our children must understand what economics are. If they have an allowance, show them how to track and account for what they earn and spend. Encourage them to think of other ways to earn money (It is called motivation.) Not teaching them to be greedy, but teaching them to be frugal and to make wise decisions about spending and earning. If you are led, share with them your family budget so they might understand that you, too, have to maintain a budget.

Teach your children how to say no. As we grow older, sometimes it's really hard to say no. There will be plenty of times that you will have to say no to your children, but be sure they understand the reasons and values behind your decisions. Pray that when the day comes that your child says no to someone, it is based on the teaching and leadership you provided; and that their response will be for their safety, or their moral values, or for others.

Teach your children everyday skills when they can handle the responsibilities like:

- Change the tire on your car
- Do the dishes
- Do the laundry
- Take out the trash
- Work in the garden (if you have one)
- How to build something

Teach your children good manners. When our children and grandchildren dine with us, we ask that mobile phones not come to the table. It does not always work, but at the table that is quality time for family, and it should not be interrupted. Nothing is so important that it cannot wait until the meal is finished. Elbows off the table and napkins in your lap. Show good table manners.

Manners also means, be on time! I cannot stand to be late for anything, as it shows poor planning on my part. Always arrive early, as it shows respect for those you are meeting. When your children are playing with others, teach them to be polite. No one wants to play with a troublemaker.

I still remember my mother telling me; "Son, when you are around adults do not speak unless spoken to." To this day, that taught me to be a good listener and to let others say what they have to say first, then provide my two cents worth. That was really good advice because I could listen to all other points of view, and after everyone was finished, the conversation would be directed to me. I guess you might say that I got the last word in at that moment. This allowed me to understand all of their viewpoints, positions, agreements, and disagreements, and it allowed me to make a more valuable contribution to the discussion because everyone else had been heard. Now I had their attention!

Setting goals is another one of those life skills important to instill into our children. If we are to be effective in teaching our children how to set goals, we must start by helping them to believe in themselves and motivate them to achieve their goals.

Growing up, I had set some goals for myself at an incredibly young age (preteen). I wanted to become an architect. After a long struggle with failure in my path, I finally achieved that goal, and today I am a registered architect in the state of NC There were other goals like playing sports, and my mother encouraged me to try out, which I did, and I participated in basketball, football, and track in high school. Those were my youthful goals. So as parents can we help our children set goals? Sure we can. Stop and spend some family time to discuss family and personal goals. Ask your children what they might want to achieve or do in the next month or year or in their future. Then work with them and help to create a chart or path by which they can see accomplishments along the path to achieve those goals, whether for the family or the individual.

Having taught in higher education for almost 40 years, I have learned many lessons. During the first week of my animation class, I would ask my freshman students to tell me where they want to be in five years. Our architecture and animation programs were two years long, so they had to think about their lives three years after they graduated. This exercise was done in class, and very soon I could identify those students who had a vision for their future and those who I had to help with their plans for the future. Someone once told me, "Make no small plans."

Teach history: Say what?! Yes! Teaching our children history is extremely important. Let us start first with your history. Share with your children your history. Tell them about yourself and your parents, and then go back as far as you can in your lineage. If you need help, there is a book called "Never Stop! Asking, discovering, and sharing!" This book can guide you with questions to ask relatives about their lives before they leave us. It also provides additional direction for the family. Your heritage is important in American history. Have you ever thought about asking your children to start a journal? One day their journal will be a historical family document to be shared and passed on to other generations. Have you started one?

As we continue on the journey of history, be certain that you also monitor what is being taught to your children. In today's time, many of our education systems are teaching abridged history, even cancelation history. You ask, what is cancelation history? Cancelation history is when important milestones in history or culture are deemphasized. For example from: https://www.vox.com/culture/2019/12/30/20879720/what-is-cancel-culture-explained-history-debate; The rise of 'cancel culture' and the idea of canceling someone coincides with a familiar pattern: A celebrity or other public figure does or says something offensive. A public backlash, often fueled by politically progressive social media, ensues. Then come the calls to cancel the person — that is, to effectively end their career or revoke their cultural cachet, whether through boycotts of their work or disciplinary action from an employer. It is ever more important now that we protect the first amendment of our Constitution:

Congress shall make no law respecting an establishment of religion, or prohibiting the free exercise thereof; or abridging the freedom of speech, or of the press; or the right of the people peaceably to assemble, and to petition the Government for a redress of grievances.

As parents, we must learn from our children that what our children are being taught and how they are being led should be in keeping with the truth and heritage of America. Use this book also, and refer to Chapter 1 as a historical guideline for those times when you can connect your children to American history in a family way.

Today as I am writing this section regarding history, it is September 11, 2020. Certainly, an important part in American history was on September 11, 2001. That was a moment in history that many Americans today remember, and many have personally experienced. On that day 19 years ago, America came under a terrorist attack that took the lives of over 3,000 people, and another 6,000 were injured. As I have looked at the news this past week, I still see terrorism occurring in America. Young people involved with Antifa are destroying property, stealing from others, shooting, beating other citizens, and burning buildings. What has happened to these young people? **We must teach and lead our children** never to intentionally cause harm to anyone, or to property! We must teach our children to be loving!

Romans 13:10, KJV
Love worketh no ill to his neighbour: therefore love is the fulfilling of the law.

As a final thought, this historical Bible verse explains very well how we can shape future events, and our children should be taught the following:

Romans 12:9-21 NIV
9 Love must be sincere. Hate what is evil; cling to what is good. 10 Be devoted to one another in love. Honor one another above yourselves. 11 Never be lacking in zeal, but keep your spiritual fervor, serving the Lord. 12 Be joyful in hope, patient in affliction, faithful in prayer. 13 Share with the Lord's people who are in need. Practice hospitality. 14 Bless those who persecute you; bless and do not curse. 15 Rejoice with those who rejoice; mourn with those who mourn. 16 Live in harmony with one another. Do not be proud but be willing to associate with people of low position. Do not be conceited. 17 Do not repay anyone evil for evil. Be careful to do what is right in the eyes of everyone. 18 If it is possible, as far as it depends on you, live at peace with everyone. 19 Do not take revenge, my dear friends, but leave room for God's wrath, for it is written: "It is mine to avenge; I will repay," says the Lord. 20 On the contrary: "If your enemy is hungry, feed him; if he is thirsty, give him something to drink. In doing this, you will heap burning coals on his head." 21 Do not be overcome by evil but overcome evil with good.

Let me now finish this section on parents and share with you a story by Robert from the North Carolina area as he shares some amazing views and perspectives on raising a family in these times. We can all learn from these lessons.

"**Leadership requires sacrifice!** This is true whether we are talking about leadership in relationship, leadership at home, or leadership at work. God designed men to be leaders over their households. You do not need look past the first couple chapters of Genesis in the Bible to see that God created man on the 6th day and gave him dominion over all living creatures (Genesis 1:26). God gave Adam the commandment to not eat from the tree in the middle of the garden before He even created Eve (Genesis 2:16). Then God created woman to be a helpmate for the man (Genesis 2:18). When Adam and Eve sinned, God called out to Adam, even though Eve was the one that was deceived by the serpent, and even though Eve disobeyed God first and then gave the fruit to Adam, God called out to Adam and it is here where we see the first example of accountability. God called out to Adam because he was the man and he was the leader; therefore, he was responsible for his actions and the woman's actions. We could stop right there and that would be controversial enough in the year 2020. Yet the simple truth about leadership remains the same. Leadership requires sacrifice. I am a husband, a father, and a deacon at our church. When my wife and I became pregnant with our first child, we began to have the conversation about what we wanted our home life to look like for our girls to grow up in.

My wife grew up in a household where her mom was a stay-at-home mom her whole life. My parents did not have that luxury, and both parents had to work. My wife grew up in private school and went to a private Christian college, while I struggled through public school and then joined the military right after high school. While having the discussion about what we wanted our home to look like, my wife communicated that she has always dreamed of being a stay-at-home mom like her mother was and then listed all the benefits that came with that lifestyle. I had just started a job with a new company, and my wife made more money than I did, but I wanted to let my wife fulfill her dream of being a stay at home mom. Over the next several months we had many discussions about it and then finally decided that my wife would work up until she couldn't work any longer due to pregnancy and then would stay-at-home after having the baby. This was a financial sacrifice, but I can now say that the benefits far exceed the sacrifice. My wife is an amazing mom to our two little girls, and they both benefit and learn from their mom. Now, as my little girls grow up, everything seems to revolve around their wants and their needs. It is important for me to continue to date my wife, but now it comes with the added cost of getting a babysitter which can be just as expensive or more than the cost of our date. This is another financial sacrifice that I accept in order to continue to pursue my wife's heart and lead her. At home, it can often feel like our lives revolve around listening to kid friendly music, reading the kids' Bible, or watching kids' TV shows such as Blue's Clues, Curious George, and more. It is important for me to take the time to take my little girls on daddy-daughter dates, read the children's Bible and the children's catechism, and practice their school material with them. In the car, they always have songs that they want to listen to as we drive. They love to listen to the Pledge of Allegiance, The Star-Spangled Banner, God Bless America, and their hymns. All of this combined results in very little time for yourself or doing things that you consider to be fun because it requires a giving up of so much of your time, but the benefit is one that will last a lifetime.

Ultimately, I want my girls to grow up in an environment where they know they are safe, loved, and cared for. I want my girls to know the Lord and grow up with a healthy view of their heavenly father. I want my girls to know how a man should treat a woman, and to see that in the way that I treat my wife and their mother, so that when they start dating, they will not settle for some guy treating them bad. I want my girls to learn from their mother how to make a home and to take care of it. All of these things and more require a daily sacrifice of giving up what I want, and even sometimes what I need, in order to shepherd my girls' hearts. It is through this daily journey that I can see how God works in their lives and in mine to take care of His children. His blessings are sprinkled all along the way in all of the cute and precious moments, whether we can capture them in a picture/video or not. He continues to bless, provide, and guide me as a husband and a father every step of the way. Ultimately, I pray that through this effort, God will get the glory and others will see through me what true leadership in the family looks like.

It is not common in the world we live in today, and a lot of the ideas and principles are becoming more and more controversial in our society. However, God's commands and promises are just as true now as they were in the time of Adam, Abraham, King David, Jesus, and Paul. As a man, a husband, and a father, I understand and accept that one day I am going to have to stand before a Holy God and give an account for how I led my life, led my wife, and led my family. That is not something that I take lightly, and while I serve a God of grace and mercy, I must run with endurance the race that is set before me, looking to Jesus, the founder and perfecter of our faith, to strengthen and guide me each step of the way."

3 John 1:4 ESV
I have no greater joy than to hear that my children are walking in the truth.

Spouses

Now I want to spend some time to focus on us. As spouses **we are the teachers and leaders to our children** and examples for others to observe. When I say we are examples for others to observe, can you recall the times when you or your spouse may have commented to each other, "Did you see what they did to their children?" Or "I would never do that to my child!" It is so difficult not to judge others. Let us focus on us. Here are some guiding principles to strengthen your relationship.

Love one another: I still remember that part of my wedding vow, "I will love and honor and cherish till death do us part." It might not have been in your wedding vow, but the principle is one of the elements that binds a successful relationship together. How does this extend further in the relationship of an American family?

- Teach each other: Can we learn from others, especially our spouses? Remember, our learning never stops. You may think this is trivial,but recently my wife taught me the proper way to make a grilled cheese sandwich. I had always depended on her to make them. First, butter one side of the bread, then grill it until it reaches the correct texture, almost toast-like. Then butter another slice of bread, lay the cheese on the first slice, put the second slice on top of it (butter side out), then flip the sandwich over till that side is toasted and the cheese is melted. Yum! Simple, but now important to me. I guess one might say I am a little tech nerdy. So, I taught my wife some computer skills. She now can set up her own zoom meetings without my help. Those are just two examples, but you get what I am trying to say.

• **Put the other first**: Remember, it's not "my way or the highway." There are times in a marriage when one needs to, out of love, concede to the wishes of the other. Just recently, I really wanted to go out for dinner. I love to eat out. My wife said she would rather stay home for dinner. Well, we stayed home for dinner. Sometimes she will put me first, and we will go out for dinner. What I am talking about here is your loving willingness to put the other first, as it is an act and display of your love and affection for the other.

• **Be a team**: Have you ever been on a team when you were younger? If you were, then you know that the goals you are trying to accomplish cannot be done alone. What are some team things you could do?

    1. Go to church together
    2. Plan a trip together
    3. Play with your kids
    4. Clean the house
    5. Work in the garden (if you have one)
    6. Pray
    7. Volunteer to help others
    8. Cook
    9. Visit someone in the hospital
    10. Teach your children

Always be willing to laugh at yourself. Have you ever done anything crazy in your family? Let me share some of our funnies. Well, the first one is we both snore at night. So, one night in bed my wife and I were lying there, and I said, "Let the games begin." She said,

"What are you talking about?" OK, here are the rules. When the first person who goes to sleep and starts snoring, the other person has to get up and go in the other room to sleep. Ha! ha! The other thing we do to laugh at ourselves is a little ritual when we go out to eat. When we get straws at the table, we take the paper around the straws and roll it up into a little ball. Then at some point during the dinner, I unexpectedly try to throw that little ball of paper down my wife's blouse, and at some point she tries to throw her's down my shirt. This even happens sometimes when we are out with friends. You should see their response. It brings a laugh!

As this chapter nears its end, let me share with you a diagram from one of my previous books, "Never Stop! Asking, discovering, and sharing!"

This diagram illustrates three interlocking rings that represent the connected links for a strong family. As a family, you have to be together in all things that you do. Beyond being together, you must provide support where it is needed. It may be to your spouse; it may be to a child; it may even be to the entire family. Then there is the ring of success, as you want everyone in the family to be successful in whatever they are trying to achieve. You are teaching and leading them to success. At the center of these three rings is a heart. Your heart and their heart make up the central force that drives everything. That heart must be strong in a Christian faith and have great love for the family and others. This will continue to make America great because of strong family principles.

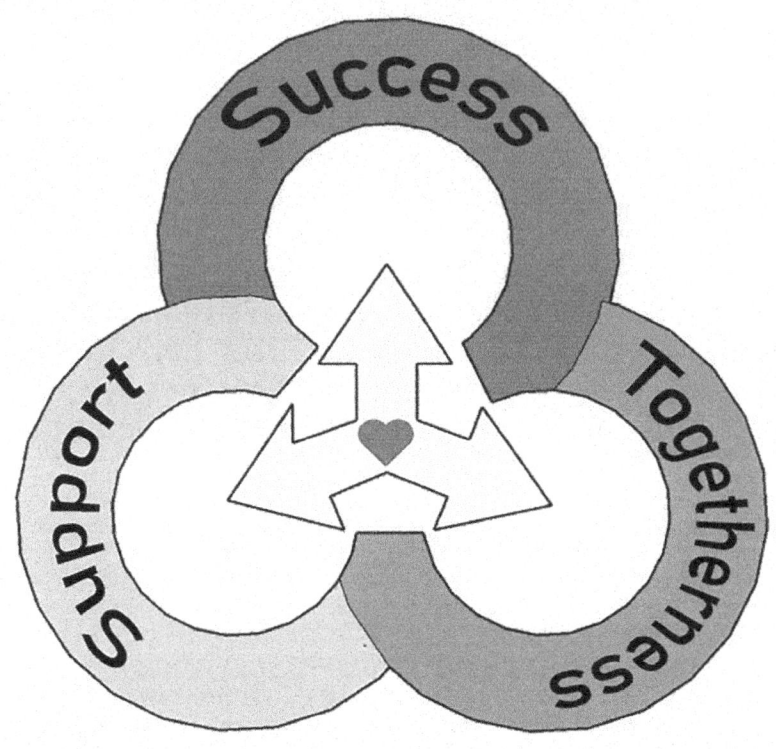

Now, if you should be in a situation where you are the only parent in the household, all of these applications still apply. Just apply the principles you just read in the section about spouses to your children as their parent and mentor. Remember whatever situation you find yourself in, take control of that situation so that you can teach and lead others to keep our founding principles from being canceled, and for our family principles to keep America great.

CHAPTER THREE

Teaching and Leading in Your Work

Take a moment and reflect on the image at the beginning of this chapter and on the cover of the book. What thoughts first come to mind! Well, first you see four silhouettes. Then you see two figures linked hand to hand. Oh! There is that other person that seems to be cheering them on or giving encouragement to the others. But wait, there is a younger looking silhouette with both arms outstretched seeking help to overcome an obstacle that faces him. It is the chasm that interferes with a desire to cross over and join the team. When I first modeled this in Daz 3D Studio, all of the figures had faces and you could tell their gender. I then took the 3D model and turned them into silhouettes to emphasize and focus on the action. What you see is a team working together to extend a hand to another and help that person continue the journey, or job, successfully. Isn't that what teaching and leading is all about? This is an exciting chapter for me as I and others will share stories and examples of what teaching and leading in your work can be like and techniques that you might consider using in the future.

Visions for Growth

As we look at our great nation in 2020 and take a moment to reflect on what is happening now and what has happened in the past, just think about the American timeline illustrated in Chapter 1. Those events were the visions people had which influenced the future of others as well as us today.

As a young child, did you have visions, desires, or excitement about what you wanted to do or become one day? I never will forget the first time that I saw a T-square in our house. I think I was probably around the age of 10 at the time. At first this thing looked like some strange miner's pick to me. When I asked what this thing was, and what it was used for, it became transformational to me. From that moment on, I had a vision of one day becoming an architect. That story is told in my previous book "Never Stop! Asking, discovering, and sharing!" The point here is that this became a vision of growth for me that was finally achieved some 27 years later.

All visions of growth do not necessarily have to be that long. To succeed with your visions for growth you must also have passion. During your life you will probably have many visions for growth. Some of those visions may not be successful, and if not and you fail, it is important that you learn what prevented that vision from being fulfilled. After I graduated from architecture school, the next part of my vision was to get a job working with an architectural firm. Well, timing could not have been worse. In 1975 the economy in the U.S. was really tough. We were in a severe recession. Unemployment was high and jobs were scarce. I remember driving to North Carolina, Tennessee, and Kentucky looking for an architectural job. Oh! By the way, one of my other visions was to teach because of some other experiences while in college. (Always have a plan B or C if plan A does not work.) So, on this job-hunting trip I stopped at about 50 to 60 architectural firms and educational institutions, filled out applications, and left resumes. When I returned to Lexington, Kentucky, in May 1975, I had not secured a job. I was married and we had one child. I had part-time work that helped a little, but my wife was also a public-school teacher. That income kept us in a rental house, and we could afford our other living expenses.

That August I was looking through the documents I had collected from all of those interviews and started to follow up to see if the firms had any new openings. No luck! However, one of the academic institutes I had stopped at had a recent vacancy, and they were looking for a senior architectural technology instructor. Long story short, I got the job and for almost 40 years I was honored to teach and lead students, faculty, and administrators.

When you are trying to set those goals for vision and growth, what might be some things to take into consideration? What about:

- •Is this an individual vision?
- •Can I do this on my own?
  Do I have the resources I need?
- •If I do not have the resources, where can I get them?
- •Will I have to relocate?
- •Will this impact others (my family)?
- •What will this cost?
- •Is the vision sustainable?
- •What is the timeline to achieve the vision?
- •Does this vision lead to another?
- •Is this a group vision?
- •Is a team required?
- •How many should be on the team?
- •How do I select team members?
- •Does the team stay together after the vision is reached?
- •What is the growth path for my vision?
- •When the vision is realized, does the vision stop?
- •Do I know your overhead and net profit?
- •Does my vision and growth need to be fed?
- •Where does my vision take me to next?
- •Do I have many visions?

What is next? At this point suggestions have involved the individual. I must admit that there are several visions I have had and have failed trying to accomplish. However, there are many more visions and growth paths that have succeeded and eventually opened other doors for success that created other visions of successful opportunities. What an honor it was for me to work in higher education at Forsyth Technical Community College in Winston-Salem, North Carolina! The next section in this chapter will expand on teaching and leading as I share about the importance of community colleges in our nation and teaching and leading the next generation.

Finding the diamonds in their Minds

This section includes a story about a teaching and leading experience that took place in the country of Ukraine. This story takes place February 2017 when I was part of an international business team (Triad Success Partners: https://triadsuccesspartners.com/), participating in a best business practices seminar on "Marketing" at the Chamber of Commerce in Lviv, Ukraine. My background is as an architect, designer, and educator with strong passions for international collaborations. During the week of our seminar, I, along with another colleague, John Moormann, were invited to speak to faculty and students at the Poly Technical National University. I was able to present the rector with a plaque honoring the university's 200th anniversary for outstanding achievements in education. John and I also toured several departments and had the honor to speak with about 80 accounting students on the meanings of being successful as students. During our classes at the chamber, one of our students was Chubai Volodymyr, an outstanding faculty member at the university and leader of "Our Perspectives Magazine". Later I returned in October to be a part of a team that would teach the importance of "Leadership in Business".

It is at this event that I was asked to submit an article for the magazine "Our Perspectives", based on my educational and leadership experiences. Volodymyr suggested I talk about the features of attracting best entrants in colleges and universities, about encouraging students to learn better, and about my teaching philosophy for education.

In the United States, a part of our unique educational process was the creation of community colleges in America. The oldest community college was founded in 1901 (Joliet Junior College in Illinois). During the Depression in the 1930s, community colleges began job-training programs to infuse needed skilled laborers into the work force. Over the years that need continues to increase, as does the number of community colleges. Some states may have only one community college, depending on the work force training needs in that state. A list of community colleges by state can be found at this link

https://en.wikipedia.org/wiki/List_of_community_colleges#United_States

Today in North Carolina there are now 58 community colleges that offer an unbelievable range of training, allied health, engineering, humanities, and social sciences, as well as math and science courses. When I was at the college, the student population at Forsyth Technical Community College was between 7,000 and 8,000. (http://www.forsythtech.edu/)

Colleges and universities have their own procedures and processes for attracting students. At Forsyth Tech, they have an open-door policy. Anyone that wants to attend the college can. Students can simply apply, and there is a testing procedure at admissions to assure and guide the students on a path for success. There are walk-in students from our state, out-of-state students, and international students (approximately 33 international students from about 11 countries). The college also has a director of recruiting whose responsibility is to expose students to the opportunities that the college has to offer. There are several tried and successful techniques to use which include, but are not limited to, the following:

- Bring middle school students (ages 10-14) to campus to tour specific curriculum areas.
- Representation at fairs and special community events.

High school students visit one of the displays at the construction trades booths. Potential students are talking with the Achitecture Program Coordinator, Professor Shoaf, to learn more about the Architecture and Interior Design programs, the curriculum, and job potentials (see Figure 1).

Figure 1
- Bring high school students (grades 9-12) to campus to tour specific curriculum areas.

(See Figure 2 on the next page). High school students posing with the mascot (Alex) of the Digital Effects and Animation program while touring the curriculum facilities.

Figure 2

- **Hosting a Summer Camp** – "Destination Forsyth Tech" Focuses on Creativity through Technology and Art.

Other attractors expose students to our educational opportunities:

- **Cost** – Students can attend a community college at much less cost than a university. "Community colleges are much cheaper than universities; in fact, the College Board reports that the average annual cost of tuition and fees for a public 2-year college are approximately $3,440 for in-district students. ... For a private 4-year university, you can expect to cough up approximately $32,410 per year in tuition and fees depending on the university chosen to attend" (source see link below).

http://study.com/blog/community-college-vs-university-the-big-differences.html

•**High School and College Credit** – Early
college students at Forsyth Tech (grades 9-12)
can attend the college and finish high school
plus earn two years of college credit in four
years (and it is free to those who qualify).
•**Finish High School** – Students can finish
high school at the college while being exposed
to a college environment.

Additionally, students have multiple pathways
for academic progress. Some students enroll with a
four-year degree in mind; two years at our college
then two more years at a university. Others might
complete a certificate 12-16 semester hours, a
one-year diploma or an associate degree, which
entales four semesters generally. As an example, a
student in the architecture program might finish
with an associate's degree and then go work with an
architectural firm, or transfer to one of the partner
universities and receive a bachelor's degree in
interior architecture, which requires only two more
years of study.

The college also provides training to
employees of local businesses through a division of
Economic and Work Force Development where the
college can create custom and specialized courses
for employees of businesses in the community,
allowing the employees to continue working while
staying current with technologies and processes.

Once the students have selected a curriculum
of study, exposure of a specialized knowledge
base will begin. As an example, I will focus on a
program I am most familiar with – Digital Effects
and Animation Technology. While working at
Forsyth Tech, I was the program coordinator and
responsible for its creation at our college. This is
only one program of many where the mining of

the diamonds in the minds of students begins. The animation program was started in 2009 and has grown to be among top attracting programs for students. This program continually has high enrollment numbers and is projected to grow at a rate of 10% per year higher than the typical job market, according to the Department of Labor and Statistics (see Figure 3).

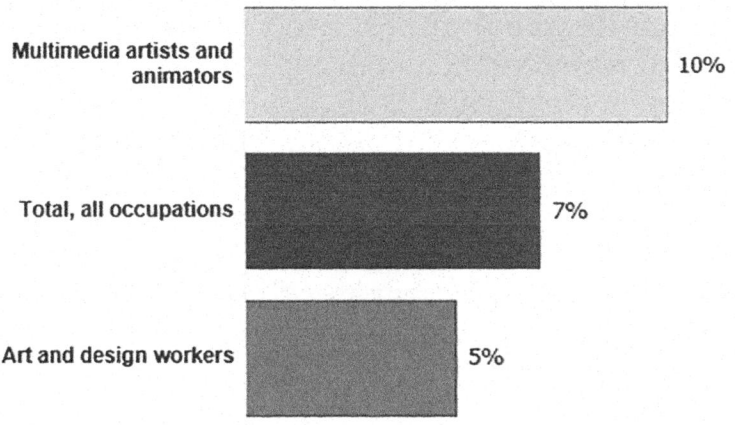

Multimedia Artists and Animators
Percent change in employment, projected 2016-26

Note: All Occupations includes all occupations in the U.S. Economy.
Source: U.S. Bureau of Labor Statistics, Employment Projections program

Figure 3

As we begin to explore this pathway, let's look at the program of study which can be found at the following link: http://www.forsythtech.edu/courses-programs/degrees/programs-a-z/digital-effects-and-animation-technology/.

In 2017 the demand was so great for this program of study that we still had to turn students away (first come first serve to get a seat in the class). There was both a day and night cohort program.

Because of our open enrollment, we attract a wide diversity of students in age and skill levels. Students may range in age from 18 to 50+. Talent level varies greatly, also. Considering that animation requires a certain level drawing capability, we might have a student that draws like a 10-year-old and some that have the skills of professional artists. **The challenge is to help the students find the diamonds in their minds** and help them each become the best they can. In this process, the goals all are reaching for are the standards required in the animation industry. Some will reach the goal and others will not.

Let us explore several processes that will help students strive for personal success and begin to search for those mental jewels they possess through advisory committees, faculty, competitions, and educational philosophies.

•**Advisory Committees**
Important to the curriculum faculty and students are advisory committees which are comprised of professionals in the industry. These committees review the works of our students and gives recommendations to the program of study if there is a need to tweak the curriculum to meet industry standards which they expect their employees to have. Many of the committee members also contribute their personal time to lecture to our students, provide demonstrations, and critique student projects. They do this on a voluntary basis because of their passions in their fields.

(See Figure 4 on the next page.) Professional animator and advisory committee members provide a lecture/demonstration to our Digital Effects and Animation students. Tony Craig is a well-known professional who has worked on many animations including "Scooby-Do" and Leroy and Stich

More of Tony's work can be found at IMBD on the link given below.

http://www.imdb.com/name/nm0186038/?ref_=nv_sr_3#producer

Figure 4

•**Faculty**:
Being connected and networked with professionals is essential, but there must be a great foundation of faculty to lead the students forward and to help them achieve personal successes. Important to training is experience. Experience in the field is extremely important. It is not how high your academic degree is, but rather what you know and can relate currently to the students. Faculty must have passion to help students to succeed. Our faculty has achieved this success as demonstrated by being the only community college in the United States in 2017 recognized as a "Toon Boom Center

of Excellence". You can see academic work of the faculty and students that were my colleagues when I taught there. These web links will provide good examples:

https://www.youtube.com/user/FTDEA/
videos?sort=dd&view=0&shelf_id=1

https://www.facebook.com/Forsyth-Tech-Digital-
Effects-Animation-200494663370118/

> •**Competitions:** It is important that students can test themselves against other students from different academic institutions. Each year the students (freshmen and sophomores) compete in our state Skills USA 3D Visualization competition: https://www.skillsusa.org/

Since the animation students began competing, they have placed 1st every year in the state competition and advanced to national competitions. It is amazing to see at the national competition the thousands of students from almost every state test their skills to be the best in America. These students are the future of an industry trained work force that makes America great.

To have successful programs and develop students that excel, I believe that faculty must also excel to be examples for their students. Having taught in higher education for over 35 years, I have had the opportunity to work with numerous students, faculty, staff, and administrators, which have fashioned and formed the evolution in my teaching philosophy. I have seen excellent professors, I have seen professors who are working only to get the monthly check. (Those professors do not last long.) Now, in reflection, I would like to share some thoughts regarding my teaching philosophy. I hope it will inspire others.

- **Philosophy**: My philosophy comes first from God, then to the heart and mind, and it is more about the evolution of a solution. For me I see that God has given me passion and vision. Those are the fuels that drive me. With passion, there is the love for what I do and a willingness to help others. Vision releases the anchor to go where I have not been. Both passion and vision strengthen me to enlighten, educate, enrich, engage, and empower students to be their best. This passion and vision are coupled with some basic precepts that help to weave together an educational philosophy that leads me to help students to "find those diamonds in their minds."

- **Investigation and Innovation**: From childhood to now; these are my seeds of discovery, and should also be the seeds for my students. I have encouraged my students to find out through investigation what the basic of a problem is, and to try to be innovative in their solution of that problem. Look at things in the way you never have before. For example, in Figure 5 on the next page an old tree stump (on the left) became inspiration to me to create a sci-fi environment on the side of a mountain with a waterfall cascading down. First came the 2D sketch then from the sketch a 3D digital model was created.

Figure 5

•**Stimulation and Motivation** are necessary when students are not stimulated and motivated. This may involve working with the student individually to develop some synergy of interest, igniting that spark of stimulation and motivation. In my intro to animation class, students were required to do one drawing every day. I would look at their work and then give them a grade based on the quality of their work. As a professional I know what a good drawing is from experience. One day a student asked why I gave a grade of C on the artwork when they thought it should be an A. "Well," I said, "it is just not that good." The student's reply was, "Well, I think it is, and so do my parents." To make a long story short, I asked one of my talented students, Britany Clark, to draw some illustrations for a rubric I developed to stimulate and motivate students to do the best they can, and help to remove much of the subjectivity in the evaluation of their art. (See Figure 6 on the next page.) Now the students could see a drawing of the same character from unacceptable to professional.

This helped to motivate a student about drawing techniques that would help them to create those diamonds in his mind to produce the best work possible.

Drawing	Description	Score
	Drawing is sloppy and no effort is present. Lacks detail, shading, and proper proportions.	0
	Drawing lacks detail, shading, and proper proportions. Line work (if present), is very sloppy. Minimal effort is present.	1
	Drawing lacks detail and may have elements out of proportion. Shading may be present, but the drawing appears two-dimensional.	2
	Drawing is shaded and exhibits attention to detail, but still has a two-dimensional quality.	3
	Shading is well done with defined attention to detail. Objects are proportional and three-dimensional.	4

Figure 6

•**Lead by Example**. Be professional in all that you do. (Others are watching.)

•**Leading leaders** is one of the more enjoyable aspects of my teaching philosophy. Team projects are an especially important part of the educational process. I believe strongly in the role to lead these leaders, with one-on-one mentoring, providing them with instruction and encouragement on how to motivate, manage, and achieve the highest expectations from their team members. As an example, in our SGD 112 class (Intro to Game Design) at a point in the semester, four or five students are selected to be hypothetical CEOs of a game company. These students have to recruit the remaining (WHAT DOES THIS MEAN?) students to join their company. Then they have to do the following:

- •Create a company logo
- •Create a new digital game concept and create it.
- •Assign responsibilities to their employees (students)
- •Keep track of all employees' time and functions on the project
- •Present the concept to potential investors (faculty)

These students could be our future leaders, and they need to learn to lead.

- **Listen and Learn.** Oh, how important this is for my educational philosophy. My learning never stops. I must be open to listen and learn from students, faculty, staff, friends, and other colleagues. I observed one of our senior students working on a video game, and he was doing some very advanced work. I asked the student where he learned how to do that because it was not taught in my class. His reply was, "I taught this to myself." Now that's passion!. I then hired that student to be my lab assistant in my next game design class. Other experiences and knowledge can only help. **One only needs to stop, listen, and learn.**
- **Excel for Excellence.** This is one of the most important factors of my educational philosophy. Having once failed academically, and never wanting to return to those experiences, again creates a life experience beneficial to students. Students, who are bordering on such a situation and have failed, but have a passion to continue, allow me the opportunity to share my failing experiences which can eventually lead to many successes. Hopefully, this encourages students to continue again and not give up on their dreams.

Remember that education never stops. You can always be a positive influence on your students, faculty, and administration. I still get cards from former students thanking me for my influence in their lives. About a year ago one of my students from 30 years ago contacted me and wanted to meet with me to listen to her thoughts on a career change and to advise her. After discussions, I was able to determine what her real passion was and encouraged her to follow that passion. I told her that if she fails, that is OK, but to never go through life and look back, regretting that she did not follow her dream. It is my hope that this information will inspire you to strive for excellence, to find excellence in yourself, and to be an educational leader for our future generation as a university professor, parent, or someone in the business and work professions.

When a country needs healing because of a financial crisis, or when America needs workers, the educational system is prepared to provide skilled students and graduates who are ready to become productive and help those they work for.

However, as Americans we must open our eyes to the types of education our students are receiving that are counter to our heritage and hurt our nation. This will be explained more in the section titled, "In these times."

Leadership in a Time of Crisis

Have you ever been in a crisis? A personal crisis, a business crisis, or a health crisis. How do you respond; what should you do? One of my first actions is to look to the Word in the Bible for comfort, and help. This verse stood out for me.

Jeremiah 29:11 ESV
For I know the plans I have for you, declares the Lord, plans for welfare and not for evil, to give you a future and a hope.

Psalm 32:8
I will instruct you and teach you in the way you should go; I will guide you with My eye.

It is comforting to know that He has a plan for

us, but that we must also be diligent with additional knowledge that prepares us to lead and last through a crisis to teach and lead another day. About 10 years ago while attending a National Community College Conference, there was an afternoon breakout session involving leading in a time of crisis. Juston C. Pate was the presenter from Maysville Community and Technical College. His session left a lasting impact on me and many of those principles I still share today with others in education and the business world, both in America and in other countries.

First, we must be able to observe or define what the crisis is and whether it is around us externally or if it is an internal crisis. Here are some situations that may define a crisis.

- **Safety is threatened**. Just look around us in these times with all of the destruction and life being taken because of sinful acts from others. I do not have to go into detail because you know exactly what I am talking about. Safety could be threatened in the workplace. A process, a policy, or other actions of employees could bring physical harm to co-workers or others.

- **Future is threatened**. What a terrible crisis indicator this could be! Definitely be on the lookout for this indicator. You would not want your roof to fall down on you and kill you! You do not want this country to become socialistic. Just look around at socialist countries and see how they are threatening the lives of others. Their future is controlled. A crisis might want to control you, but it is up to you to respond so that this is no longer a threat, which might mean making an adjustment in your family, looking for another job, or stepping up and leading through the crisis.

- **Financial structure is weakened**. I remember surviving several financial downturns. First there was the economy during President Carter's term in office, then the recession during President Obama's term in office, and more recently the sudden economic job shock to America because of the China virus.
- **Integrity is shaken**. Integrity is one of the most important values we can have. I have told my children that if you lose everything, the only things you have left of value are honesty, love, and integrity. In these times we do not have to look far to discover those that have shaken our integrity. Just look at the federal government and observe all of the deception and lies that have taken place with the false impeachment of our president. Just look at those who use others just for their benefits. That is integrity lost. You probably know someone who has lost integrity. Hopefully, as we progress in this chapter you will see traits and principles that will help you to lead in a crisis.
- **Environmental disaster has occurred**. Again, I say we just have to look around in these times and we can see many environmental disasters. These are more easily recognized: fires, hurricanes, earthquakes; human pollution of the air, water, and soil.

Once a crisis has been identified we must begin to determine our responses. These responses happen at two different levels.

- **External Level**: At this level one has to deal with logistics of the crisis. What is the structure of the existing situation, what personnel are available to help, and what is the plan?

•**Internal Level**: This is you! Is your character and are your values established so that others can have confidence in you? What is your resolve? Do you have the will power to lead through the crisis? Is your emotional capacity sufficient to deal with conflicts and pressures that may continue to attack you as you lead through a crisis? This internal factor is extremely important as it will drive your behavior on that path to lead in a time of crisis.

During a time of crisis, what are some of the qualities and responses required to help you and others endure and survive that crisis? Let's now take a specific look at those qualities required of a leader, or an institution, whether it be educational, business, religious, or of a personal nature. The following list will provide you with an option for consideration to strengthen or add to your plan of action.

•**Accurate Information**: Absolutely a must! When a crisis hits, it is usually unexpected. There can also be signs of an upcoming crisis as well. Whichever is the case, you must have accurate information. Be sure that the information is verifiable. If you try to solve a crisis with inaccurate information, it is certainly going to create another crisis. You want others, as well, to believe in your information.

•**Understand the underlying factors/evidence.** Just look at the pandemic of 2020 (the China virus). What were the underlying factors that caused the spread of the virus? What was the evidence of its creation? In business, it might be that you grew your business too rapidly and now your growth cannot be covered by the income (crisis in the making). So as someone once told me, "Get your facts right, then come and talk to me."

- **Communication**: If you are the person leading an institution through and out of a crisis, you must keep the communication channels open. For some it might be letting them know every detail that is taking place. For others it might be on a need-to-know basis. By this I am implying that they know what the big picture is and that a plan is in place progressing towards an equitable outcome.

- **Visible Leadership**: A great example is our recent pandemic. President Trump rapidly created a national response team. This team remained visible nationally on a fairly regular schedule, updating us on their actions as they helped us work through this crisis. Some may or may not agree with the details, but nevertheless there was a confidence in the leadership that provided levels of security, hope, and normalcy for those affected by the crisis.

- **Transparency, Integrity, and Trust**: The most important factors an institution must have whether in a crisis or not are these three. If those around you do not see these traits, why should they have confidence that you will successfully help through a crisis? The institution must not be hypocritical. It must not say you will be led in this direction, but later you find out that you were actually led in another direction, and they only needed your temporary support. Do not be like many politicians who say one thing to get your vote, yet later not do what they told you they would do. This may be one of the

most important directives or
traits to help one through a crisis. This also
brings to mind several scriptures:

Proverbs 4:25-27 NIV
25 Let your eyes look straight ahead; fix your gaze directly before you. 26 Give careful thought to the paths for your feet and be steadfast in all your ways. 27 Do not turn to the right or the left; keep your foot from evil.

Proverbs 11:3
3 The integrity of the upright guides them, but the unfaithful are destroyed by their duplicity.

Proverbs 12:22
22 The LORD detests lying lips, but he delights in people who are trustworthy.

- **Flexibility and Balance**: Wow! How important is this! Just look around in 2020 at the flexiblity and balance eveyone is having to navigate and maintain. What a test year for all of us! Talk about teaching and leading, this is the year of revelation of flexibility and balance. I don't need to say much about this as there are so many examples all around us that we are learning from. Teachers have to learn new technologies to conduct remote classes. Many business employees are required to work remotely, wearing masks, and social distancing. Not just people working for institutions understand what flexibility and balance is during a crisis. All of America understands this.

- **Prepared**: Have a plan. No crisis can successfully be mitigated without a plan. Of course, there

is the master plan. For example, develop
a cure for a pandemic. However, that master
plan must also be specific in its details
to achieve the original vision plan. As an
architect, when I design a building it consists
of the general plans (floor plans and
elevations), but before the vision of that
building can take place, all of the details must
be included for its construction.

Luke 14:28-33 ESV
*For which of you, desiring to build a tower, does not first
sit down and count the cost, whether he   has   enough
to complete it? Otherwise, when he has laid a foundation
and is not able to finish, all who see it begin to mock him,
saying, 'This man began to build and was not able to finish.'
Or what king, going out to encounter another king in war,
will not sit down first and deliberate whether he is able
with ten thousand to meet him who comes against him with
twenty thousand? And if not, while the other is yet a great
way off, he sends a delegation and asks for terms of peace. ...*

- **Spend time learning.** This takes us back
  to the beginning bullet point regarding
  accurate information. You must spend the
  time necessary to learn all that you can about
  the crisis. Learn about those involved. Learn
  about what the cost effects are, learn about
  those who can help you, learn about
  those things that can harm you. This learning
  process will enable you to collect the accurate
  information necessary to proceed.

Now that you understand many of the factors
that are required for institutions to begin to do and
serve in response to a crisis, there are also some
very important individual characteristics and

understandings that you must possess to lead.

- **Fearless Passion of Responsibility**: Leading during a crisis is not for the weak minded or faint of heart. Perhaps because of the position you are in, there is no other choice, and as they say, "The buck stops with you." It might be a situation where you will have to stand up or be the one that leads others into battle. Whatever the situation, it means that you are taking personal responsibility and leadership for the actions that are about to take place. It means that you have the resolve to withstand whatever is in your path that will stop you from victory, and that you are willing to take responsibility for your actions and the cause-and-effects they might have on others. Wow! This could be you one day.
- **Calmness**: Can you be calm in the midst of a crisis or a storm? Some of you may have experienced unsettling situations. Your calmness can be a signal and a beacon for others to be calm also. Jane Burnett describes six ways to stay calm in a crisis.
  1. **Do not lose it**. Do not lose your temper. It tells others you can be trusted with responsibility. Even if you lose control only once, people will remember that one time you were not calm, and it could erase most of your goodwill with them. A few Bible verses can help you to stay calm in a crisis:

Proverbs 15:1 ESV
A soft answer turns away wrath, but a harsh word stirs up anger.

Psalm 37:8
Calm your anger and abandon wrath. Do not be angry — it only leads to evil.

Matthew 6:27
And who of you by being worried can add a single hour to his life?

2. **Do not try to take on the emotions of others.** Have you ever watched a news cast and was drawn into the emotion of that event? Have you been in a meeting when others were screaming and upset about something? You cannot be a sponge and draw in those emotions. You can have compassion and concern from those exposures, but a true leader will need to be insulated in a way that those emotions do not cause change but that the facts cause change.

Galatians 5:22-23 ESV
But the fruit of the Spirit is love, joy, peace, patience, kindness, goodness, faithfulness, gentleness, self-control; against such things there is no law.

3. **Remember it's all in how you communicate.** Jane Burnett said, "When you are angry, there can be a tendency to be sarcastic for some people, or passive-aggressive for others. Be aware of the intentions and emotions you are directing at other people. Not everyone is — or should be — understanding or accepting of anger, ranting, or silence. You don't

want to burn any bridges, especially if you don't know the colleague well and they could carry reports of your behavior through the company." Remember, once you have said something you cannot take it back. Think twice, but speak once.

4. **Focus on your breathing**. After having triple bypass heart surgery in 2013, I learned while going through rehab how to breathe as a means to reduce stress. Begin by inhaling through your nostrils (3 seconds), hold your breath (2 seconds), and allow a long exhale through your mouth (4 seconds). It was calming for me.

5. **Remove yourself from the situation.** If you are in a hostile environment, be prepared to walk away for a moment. Take a time out. Think of something that will put you in a different frame of mind. Let the calming environment return before reengaging.

6. **Think about what you can control.** Most importantly, realize that some things are out of your control. Realize that those are responsibilities of others and let them take action, as necessary. The sooner you let go, the sooner it will reduce your stress and aid you in remaining calm in a crisis.

• **Vision**. For me personally, vision is one of the thriving and driving forces in life. Without vision how can a leader lead? All leaders must have a vision plan during a time of crisis, as mentioned earlier. This is the most difficult skill for leaders. Some have it, and some do not. When you do find a person of vision, watch them and learn from them.

• **Lead by example.** You would be amazed to discover all of the people that are looking at you and what you do, not only in your work environment but in everything. I remember a time that I gave my Digital Effects and Animation students an incredibly challenging assignment. I could see they were struggling with that assignment. So, I sat down at a computer in the lab where they were working and did that same assignment they had. The students could see what I was doing and gained inspiration and knowledge as we all worked on the same goal. Even what you do as a leader can be shared with others who saw HOW you lead. Never be fearful of taking on a leadership role.

• **Self-awareness:** Know what your strengths and weaknesses are. This is extremely important if you are to become a successful leader. If someone is better than you at doing something during a crisis, recruit them to be a part of a team that can bring success to the situation.

When taking leadership training with others at Forsyth Tech, we were sent to The Center for Creative Leadership, where strengths and weaknesses as a leader could be evaluated (ccl.org). Before attending, those you supervised were given a form to evaluate you, and those that supervised you were given a form to evaluate you. Then you attended their classes, and when finished they provided you with a personal assessment of your leadership strengths and weaknesses. Truly, this was an amazing experience for me.

- **Empathetic:** It is important to understand the needs of other. As a team leader, the question is not what can you do for me, but what can I do for you to make what you are involved in more successful. **How can I help you**? If someone is coming to you with a crisis situation, give them your full attention. Put all other things aside and give them the feeling that they have your undivided attention. By providing your full attention to the problem it means that you are beginning to understand the problem. Then you can make the plans necessary for the success that is required. A quote from Theodore Roosevelt: "Nobody cares how much you know, until they know how much you care."
- **Management Skills:** To be successful at anything you have to have good management skills. Many books have been written just on this topic. I remember one time someone asked me what I did at Forsyth Tech. At that time in my career my response was, "Well I am the Interim Dean of Engineering, responsible for overseeing budgets and faculty for 34 curriculum programs of study, and Department Chair for Design Technologies, which includes Architecture, Interior Design, Broadcast Production Technology, and Digital Effects Program. Also, I am the Program Coordinator for the

Animation program and teach two classes in that program. Additionally, I am the colleges' coordinator for International Partnerships, and co-chair of our international committee; and I am on the V.P.'s academic advisory team." His response was Whaaaat? How can you handle all of that? My response was that I am a good juggler and manager. I managed it all by His grace.

Luke 12:48 NIV
From everyone who has been given much, much will be demanded; and from the one who has been entrusted with much, much more will be asked.

Now you have been provided with thoughts, guidelines, and procedures, skill sets necessary to form a foundation that might help your leadership in a time of crisis. In America, now, we need teachers and godly leaders who can begin to heal the many crisis situations that have embedded themselves in our schools, our politics, and our communities. Do not just take my words and thoughts on leadership skills, as you will read in this next section the words and lessons from other leaders in America.

Lessons from Leaders

I really get excited when a section like this starts. This is where you get to read viewpoints from others about "Teaching and Leading." Here, as the old saying goes, is where "the rubber meets the road". What better way than to be presented with important lessons from other leaders. These leaders cross many types of professions. You will hear from educators, pastors, CEOs of businesses, as they share with you examples based on their life experiences involving training and leadership, and the importance of a lesson learned. We might be able to apply these in our daily lives or our businesses. Let us begin.

Once Upon A Time

By
Captain James Kinney, USN (ret)

Once upon a time there was a man from Kansas who was given an opportunity to go to Kenya on the east coast of Africa on the Indian Ocean. This man was a very ordinary man with a wife and children and grandchildren. He had a successful career and a life worth living.

Given the chance to pursue a Kingdom challenge and go to Kenya to travel in the bush and meet people very different from those in his everyday circle of life, he was thrilled to go, but apprehensive of what he would find ... how he would react ... how he would be received. He was venturing far beyond his comfort zone.

The plan was to travel to the bush country north and west of Mombasa to help a local pastor plant a church in an area of significant Muslim influence. Each day, his team of three, himself, a Kenyan native translator ... most of the people he would meet spoke Swahili ... and a lady from New Jersey who volunteered to join the effort, ventured out with us on this mission trip.

The man from Kansas was, at each village they visited, to gather a crowd and to tell the story of the earth's history to as many in each village as would listen. So, for several days, each morning the small team would be dropped off in a designated area and hike to as many villages as were accessible to them geographically that day. At every village they visited, their first responsibility was to get the permission of the leader of the village to hold a meeting with his people.

One day they were told before they left for their trek through the bush, that one of the villages they would be visiting was led by the son of a man who was known for his influence and for Muslim convictions which included strong anti-Christian beliefs.

The man from Kansas was told by the mission organizers that they did not really know what kind of reception the team would receive when they entered the village. Not really fearful ... but certainly a little hesitant when approaching the village, they were met by a well-built and obviously well-conditioned man in his young 30s. While his countenance was clouded as to the reason for the team's visit, it was explained, and he was asked his permission to tell the villagers who were available the story of the earth.

The leader's response was more curious than hostile, but wasn't truly welcoming, but he allowed the team to set up in the middle of the village while he assembled a crowd and sent runners out to bring the workers from the fields. It was not a large village, so the assembled crowd may have numbered 30. The head man and his very pregnant wife took seats in the very front of the assembly to hear what this strange white man from Kansas had to say.

He told the head man and those gathered about a Creator who had formed the earth and all that was in it. How He had created the perfect garden and placed a man and a woman in the garden to enjoy its fruits and to fellowship with the Creator Himself.

The white man from Kansas shared how the first man and woman had decided they could probably make things better for themselves, so they rebelled against the Creator. As a result, the Creator removed them from the perfection of His garden and told them they would now have to work the soil themselves in order to eat and survive. Their fellowship with the Creator was broken and life became difficult and full of sorrow.

The Creator loved the man and woman whom He had designed to live forever with Him, but as a result of their rebellion, they could not return to the garden until they had been reconciled with their Creator.

Man's rebellion or "sin" was so complete that it infected all the children of man since that day of rebellion to this. We are all guilty of our own sin. The Creator's word tells us that we have all sinned and the result of our sin is separation from the great plans the Creator has for all the children of man. He wants to enjoy fellowship with us and to give us an eternity of blessings.

But the Creator's word tells us that all men have sinned and earned the righteous judgment of death. How could this separation caused by our sin be overcome and justice be served?

In His great love for each of us, the Creator sent His Son to earth to pay the penalty of sin so that we could be reconciled to His Father. So, Jesus, the son of the Creator, came to earth as a man, lived without sin so that He Himself was not guilty of rebellion and could be the perfect sacrifice for our sins so that our sins would be forgiven, having been paid for by the Creator's own son, Jesus Himself. Once forgiven, we can be restored to a perfect relationship with our Creator and spend eternity with Him.

As a result of sin, we will all die physically, but our spirit will live forever in heaven with our Creator.

The Kansan, working all this time through the translator, then asked the village gathered if they would like to be forgiven of their rebellion against the Creator. And as they bowed together there in the small village, the man from Kansas led a short prayer of acknowledgment of their personal sin, repentance and asking the Creator to restore them to Himself for all eternity.

Something amazing happened at this point that had not happened in any other village the Kansan visited either before or after this moment.

The villagers were all asked to repeat the prayer as the translator led them. Usually there were many who prayed, but their voices were low and indistinguishable. This day, when asked to reach out to the Creator, the village head, boldly in a loud voice proclaimed,

"I AM A SINNER ... I NEED FORGIVENESS ... JESUS PLEASE FORGIVE ME ... I SURRENDER TO YOU ... I WANT TO SPEND ETERNITY WITH YOU IN HEAVEN!"

The chieftain's wife also prayed. She was "great

with child," and the village head asked the Kansan if he would say a prayer of blessing over his pregnant wife and soon-to-be-born son.

It was an incredibly special time; it seemed the sun stood still for a moment as heaven rejoiced over this miracle. A team of strange white folks from thousands of miles away show up on the plains of Kilimanjaro by divine appointment ... Wow ... what a God!

BUT THAT'S NOT THE END OF THE STORY.

The next day, the team is miles away at another village when a runner from the village of yesterday's miracle shows up with a message from the head man. His wife had delivered the night before and he wanted the Kansan and the team to return and pronounce a blessing on his newborn son and to give him the Kansan's name. According to the translator, this was an unheard-of event in that culture.

Arriving back in the small village, the team found mother and child both healthy and alert – this young man born on the dirt floor of a Kenyan hut. The man from Kansas offered a simple blessing for mother and child, then gave the newborn the name James ... not after the Kansan, but after the brother of Christ and asked the Creator to give this young man ministry influence worthy of his name.

This birth reminds us another birth 2,000 years ago ... a miraculous birth meant to save mankind from the just deserved penalty for his sin.

Thank you Heavenly Father for loving us so much! We can all be teachers and leaders if we are willing to leave our "comfort zones." We can help heal America if only we do it with Him and through Him.

About
Captain James Kinney, USN (ret)

NAVY CAREER: 1968-1993
• Held three command posts
• Served on the Joint Chiefs of Staff
• As Mission Commander, flew both tactical and strategic reconnaissance missions from 9 aircraft carriers
• Transitioned the Department of Defense from paper & pencil recruit testing to computer adaptive testing for all services for all enlisted applicants
• Highly decorated, culminated by receipt of the highest peacetime award offered by the U.S. military

BUSINESS CAREER:
1993-2003
• Vice President Walk Thru the Bible
1993-2004
• Led turnaround of non-profit seminar ministry team
• Redesigned business model
• Moved division from donor supported to self-sustaining
• Expanded annual events by 400%
• Doubled annual revenue

2003-2007   Calvary Baptist Church
• Managed major staff reorganization
• Led church from single campus to multisite
  ministry Transitioned printing plant to
  21st-century technology

2007-2008 Huckabee for President campaign
               staff
2008-present
• Founder and CEO of Inspire and Ignite consulting
  firm
• Most prominent client has been Convention of
  States

2009-2014
• Wrote and produced a daily political commentary,
  "Inspire and Ignite" radio broadcast syndicated on
  more than 100 radio stations across the country

Authored two books addressing the need for a
conservative resurgence in America

Currently-Editorial writer for local weeklies

The role of Mistakes and History in Teaching and Learning

By
Bob Hicks

George Wilhelm Friedrich Hegel, a German idealist philosopher of the late 18th and early 19th century, gave us an important truth about teaching and learning. He is attributed with the often-repeated statement, "the only thing we learn from history is that we learn nothing from history." What we can agree with in Hegel's point is that we see people, institutions, governments, and societies making the same mistakes, falling into the same traps, over and over again. Certainly, if we do not learn from the mistakes of our past, we will surely commit them again.

The Old Testament is replete with examples of this repetition. The story of Gideon in the Book of Judges testifies to the reoccurring practice of the Hebrew people falling away from obeying the Lord, compromising their faith in the One True God by assimilating the gods and cultures of pagan neighbors. They would suffer subjugation to and dominance by those neighbors until God in His mercy would raise a leader to expel the idol worship and break the bonds of suffering at the hands of people who did not honor Him. Gideon was one of thirteen such leaders during a short but formidable period in Israel's history whose story is told in Judges, chapters six through nine. But Gideon's story begins and ends with the frequently repeated assessment of God's people, leader after leader, time after time: "Again the Israelites did evil in the eyes of the Lord" (6:1, 10:6). The Bible's books of history and the Prophets simply support this reoccurrence. Generation after generation from before Gideon until in our own time, nations have not learned of the suffering, death, destruction, and costs of war. The Great War—the so-called "war to end all wars" — only created the causes to fight another, even larger, more horrific, and deadlier war less than twenty years later.

The "dust bowl" agricultural disaster of the 1920s and '30s seem to be reappearing these recent years for much the same causes in America's great vegetable growing region of the country's southwest. On a much more personal basis, the tragic, painful and costly lessons of the life-robbing practice of smoking cigarettes by their parents and grandparents appear lost to today's youth who vape. Each year countless lives are lost in automobile accidents as a result from driving under the influence, speeding, running red lights and stop signs. Consider the heartache of loved ones whose child found the loaded gun without a trigger lock, or the senseless shootings, all of which are attempts "to even the score," prove a point, or to satisfy a revengeful spirit. George Santayana, a Spanish American essayist, poet and novelist who lived until the early 1950s, paralleled Hegel's thought with the statements, "Those who cannot learn from history are doomed to repeat it", and "Only the dead have seen the end of war!"

Yet, it is true that we can learn from our past and

mistakes. In the New Testament there are number of examples of persons who, by gaining a new insight into their thoughts and deeds, learned how to relate to others, even teach others how their lives could be changed for the better. Chapter nineteen of the Gospel of Luke tells the story of the transformation of a tax collector named Zacchaeus. Coming to terms with his fraudulent work, he made amends with those whom he had cheated, robbed, and taken advantage. The story of Peter's denials in John 18 and then the conviction with which he preached to the crowd gathered in Jerusalem on the Day of Pentecost (Acts 2) is another illustration. No doubt the greatest example is that of a man named Saul, a Pharisee, whose name not only changed to Paul, but whose life turned from persecution of the church to its most avid promotor, developer, and supporter (The Book of Acts, chapters 8-28).

The common thread through each of these stories is the redemption from their past brought by Jesus Christ. He opened their eyes, their hearts, to what they had been doing in their lives – their history ¬ and what they mistakenly believed, talked about, and supported, so that they could learn how to live differently, relate to others on a whole different plain, and live their lives more abundantly, joyfully. By the work of the Holy Spirit and faith in Jesus, the Christ, God enables us to learn from our mistakes, our history of selfishness and self-centeredness, to experience a whole new dimension of living. It is the one He intended for us to experience with our creation and one that He blesses without end.

Certainly, my life experience is rich with failures, mistakes, misunderstandings, some of which were powerful lessons learned and taught resulting in more positive endings. During my career as a minister and church pastor, the mistakes I made in one church prevented me from repeating them when I moved on to a new parish. Pastors are oftentimes held to a higher standard than their parishioners or the general populace. But we are not perfect; we have our faults of being human too, and if we are humble enough to admit it, we are always in the need of grace. I have said things I should not have said, not only as a pastor, but also as a Christian, compromising my witness as a disciple of Christ and a servant of the Lord. I have expressed anger, resentment, selfishness, pride, discontentment, and prejudice. I have demanded my own way many times throughout my career. My family has suffered the consequences far too often.

My tenure with a congregation ended in too short a period as church leaders and members lost confidence in my leadership and were hurt. But in many such situations there was for me my loving wife to gently counsel me to learn from my mistake, or the courageous elder or deacon who, like Nathan who confronted David after the King's affair with Bathsheba and the murder of her husband, Uriah (II Samuel 11, 12), opened my eyes to see what I could not but others could in my behavior, leadership, and witness. There was also, always, the merciful love of Him Who called me to serve as a church pastor and minister of His Word. God has dealt with me in an abundance of redeeming grace to make humility a much greater ingredient in my relations with others so that my ministry was far more helpful to them and to the community I sought to serve. Becoming aware of my mistakes and tendencies to misinterpret others' words, motives, and values in my past, by the grace of God, has taught me to respond to hurting people with greater compassion, to confused and misdirected people with less judgment and better understanding, to the distraught and discouraged with greater encouragement and the hope of my faith in Jesus Christ.

History can be a great teacher if we learn from it. Mistakes are often painful but necessary lessons that can bring redeeming change resulting in improvement and better consequences. The Bible proclaims the truth that God forgives our mistakes, our failures, our wrongdoing and sin when we acknowledge them (I John 1:9), change, and seek to do differently. In the end, a quotation my wife expressed very often in our early years of marriage rings true still, "Be patient with me; God is still working!" He never has given up on me. After fifty years of marriage — with lots of mistakes, failures, disappointments, and disagreements — such a history is blotted away with three other words that also ring true still, "I love you."

About
Bob Hicks

- A native of Lexington, KY, presently a resident of Hendersonville, NC
- Married with two adult children, four grand children
- Graduated from Transylvania University in 1971 with a BA in Philosophy of Religion
- Graduated in 1974 from Lexington
- Theological Seminary with a Master of Divinity
- Ordained a Minister of the Gospel by the Christian Church (Disciples of Christ), in 1974 served congregations in Kentucky, Virginia, North Carolina, and Indiana until 2015
- Guest evangelist in Sao Paulo, Brazil, twice, 1990 and 1991, Mission leader to Augucalalentes, Mexico, and Costa Rico 1995 and 2000
- Served as Construction Manager and Executive Director of Habitat for Humanity affiliates in Kentucky, Florida, and Georgia from 1999-2011
- Volunteer fire fighter from 1971 to present, honored twice for service and life saves
- Certified by North Carolina as an Emergency Medical Technician in 2015, serving until present

Leadership

By
Jack Bales

In my 37 years of working in the insurance industry, I had many supervisors and regional managers. Over that time, I noticed a couple of traits that nearly all companies followed:

1. When looking for those whom they considered promotable management material, they would normally look within the company for those who exhibited the best technical expertise – in other words, those who appeared to be exceptional at doing their current jobs.

2. In order to shake things up and try to do things differently and better, many companies went outside their own staffs to try and attract successful candidates from other companies who were considered (at least in the profit and loss ledger) to be better run.

Often times, these folks were indeed exceptional at their jobs, and some of the time they produced the desired results, that is, a better bottom line. The problem, at least from my perspective, was that the people hired or promoted almost never displayed what I would call "people skills." Yes, they knew their product or market sector or how to squeeze the most out of employees, but most of the time the employees became unhappy or unfulfilled in their respective jobs. Many would opt to leave the company for what they considered to be greener pastures, even for less money.

I was told by some friends in the human resources department that it was expensive to attract and train new employees. At the same time, it seemed rare to find employees who would make a career and stay with the company long term. So, it was an endless cycle of hiring new employees and training them, only to have them go somewhere else.

To be sure, it will always be necessary to attract and train new employees. Even if every employee did stay for 30 years, they would eventually retire, move, get married, or die. Even though there is no way to get around this, still a company could save a lot of money simply by making it extremely attractive to stay long term.

As I mentioned earlier, most great technicians make poor managers. Why is this? It is because they do not have training in the art of developing their staffs or don't care to even try. Having managerial authority, at least for some, can swell a person's pride and sense of self-worth to a level that becomes difficult for those under their authority to deal with.

I will give an example. There were three levels of management in a branch office at the company where I started when I got out of college in 1978. There was the General Manager, the Department Manager, and then my Immediate Supervisor. When I was hired, I was interviewed by the person who would become my Immediate Supervisor first, then the Department Manager on the second interview. I immediately noticed a stark difference between the Department Manager and my Immediate Supervisor.

Naturally, every person has their own personality and style. What made the difference for me was how I was looked at and treated by each. My first interview with the person who would become my Immediate Supervisor was fairly cold and very businesslike. I was amazed when I was called back for the second interview and walked into the Department Manager's office. As I walked in, he stood, walked over to me, put his arm on my shoulder, and warmly welcomed me into his office. Immediately, I was at ease and the interview went well enough that he hired me on the spot.

Later, when I started to work and learned the company history of the two men, I quickly saw that my Immediate Supervisor had been promoted because he was a great technician. He knew the insurance policy inside and out and how to underwrite an insurance risk to perfection.

On the other hand, the Department Manager had never done the job of an insurance underwriter. He had come over from the (at the time) defunct Marketing Department and had virtually no idea of the in's and outs of risk selection and exactly how policies were issued through the computer. Consequently, he had to lean on the Immediate Supervisor to help him deal with what he did not understand about the nuts and bolts of the operation. But, he had great people skills and everybody loved him. Virtually no one liked the Immediate Supervisor even though he knew the job better than anyone within the department. As a result, very few new employees would stay for very long.

Much later, when I was asked to evaluate the two men, I pointed out that the number one personnel mistake of the company was to put technical skill over people skill when it came to hiring/recruiting managers/supervisors.

The conclusion to draw from this, no matter what the vocation, is that the most successful leaders have people skills from which to draw. Naturally, no one is born with this information. It is an acquired skill over time. The Bible refers to this as "wisdom."

To anyone who aspires to be a leader, the very first place they should start is asking God to give them wisdom. James 1:5 NKJV; "If any of you lacks wisdom, let him ask of God, who gives to all liberally and without reproach, and it will be given to him".

Exodus 31:6 includes more information about what God can do if asked.

Exodus 31:1-3 NKJV

1 Then the LORD spoke to Moses, saying: 2 "See, I have called by name Bezalel the son of Uri, the son of Hur, of the tribe of Judah. 3 And I have filled him with the Spirit of God, in wisdom, in understanding, in knowledge, and in all manner of workmanship."

God can supply not only wisdom, but abilities and skills to get a job done.

The next thing that I think makes a great leader is integrity. Mark Twain is quoted as having said, "Always do right. It will gratify some people and astonish the rest." In our day, people are craving leadership that is honest and does not have to depend on lies and half-truths to attract a following. In his book, "The Little Red Book of Wisdom," Mark DeMoss points out that in his experience of going door to door selling books, the one thing he discovered is that "customers often buy the person selling rather than the product." A lot of people can smell a con job right up front. Whether it's selling encyclopedias door to door or building a successful enterprise of any kind, being honest and sincerely caring about people is key. Just as it was for me being warmly invited into a manager's office.

About
Jack Bales

Jack came to Christ at the age of 11. At 16, he felt called to go into some kind of Christian Ministry. As a result of this, he was given the opportunity to preach at various churches and youth meetings around the state of Florida where he was living at the time. After graduating high school, he worked for a few years at various jobs to earn money to go to college. Jack chose Free Will Baptist Bible College (now Welch College) to do his undergraduate studies, while also taking classes at Belmont University and Fort Wayne Bible College. Jack graduated in 1978 with a B.S. degree, having majored in Bible & Elementary Education. For the next 37 years, he would work in the insurance industry in various roles in the underwriting, marketing, sales and claim departments, all the while, being involved with the ministry of teaching, and sometimes filling in for vacationing pastors.

In the early 2000s, after a series of revival meetings, Jack felt led to begin graduate studies at Trinity Theological Seminary, concentrating on Christian Apologetics. Jack finished his studies in June of 2011.

From 1975 until now, Jack began building a theological library that now consists of almost 1,000 volumes. Jack completed a book entitled "Thy Kingdom Come" in 2002 which remains unpublished. He currently is rewriting some chapters and hopes to publish it soon. His hobbies are fishing, camping, target shooting, flying model airplanes, and performing magic (illusion) shows. Jack has been married to America Bales for 45 years. Jack now teaches a Sunday school class and Bible study at Calvary Baptist Church, and is a host of a popular podcast series called "Three Men for Thee" https://3-mft.fireside.fm/. He and his wife, Meky, have one daughter and one grandson.

Serving Others

By
Anita Teague

In the state of Tennessee, Friday the 13th of March in 2020 will forever be remembered as the day life changed and we all went home. It was the last day schools were open for the remainder of that school year, and for those people who were lucky, the day they took everything home from work to set up home office. For many others, however, it was the last day of income they would receive for weeks or even months. Friday the 13th of March 2020 is the day Tennessee pretty much shut down due to the COVID-19 pandemic.

As the executive director of a non-profit agency that serves people with intellectual and developmental disabilities, March 13th stands out as the date my leadership team and I decided to send all of our staff across the region home to work remotely. A lot of the people we serve also have complex medical conditions, and many of the babies in our early intervention program have come home from the neonatal intensive care unit. The data has shown that people with disabilities might contract the virus at the same rate as the entire population, but the death rate is four times higher. Needless to say, we quickly developed a plan to provide teletherapy and complete home and provider visits remotely, using the phone and/or video conferencing.

For many of the families we serve and support,

life is already full of hard choices – having only one parent work outside the home so the other parent can care for the family member with the disability; having to make the choice between paying for heat in the winter or filling your child's required prescriptions; having to decide on paying for gas to take your child to all their needed therapies or pay for groceries. COVID-19 only made the choices become harder and harder.

At the end of July, Governor Lee (the Tennessee governor) announced the Tennessee Community CARES program, which would grant $150 million to Tennessee non-profits to provide COVID relief to Tennesseans. There was no question – to me or to my leadership team – we were going to apply! Through conversations with my team, we were able to determine what supports we could provide. Listening to their ideas and their passion to help others, I was able to suggest broadening our agency's mission to serve all individuals with ANY type of disability, and their families. This is the direction we decided to pursue, and we quickly submitted our grant proposal. On September 2, 2020, we found out that we were awarded the VERY large grant to provide food relief, technology assistance, behavior supports, emergency living funds, and PPE to families in 13 of our most rural counties. And, we had to spend all of our funds by November 15th!!! Let the fun begin!

One of my favorite leadership sayings is that I will not ask any of my staff to do something I am not willing to do myself – so this additional program, albeit short-term, was going to be developed, implemented, and managed by myself and one of my program coordinators. Although there is a very important aspect to delegation, and I must say I am pretty good with delegation without micromanaging, there is a time and a place where you also must lead by example and recognize that if there is extra work to be completed, you must push up your sleeves and jump right up to your knees in the added responsibilities. So, I started working 60-plus hour work weeks (with a one hour commute each way) to get this new program off the ground and to start serving those who had been negatively impacted by COVID, so my other staff would not have to work significantly more hours than a normal work week.

This short-term grant gave us the ability to serve those impacted by COVID, while at the same time, it gave me the opportunity to serve my staff by taking up the extra burden of working longer and harder hours so they would not have to work too many more than usual. This opportunity has allowed our agency to reach out and serve those who are in need, even more than we already do with our established programs. "To whom much is given, much is expected" ... and as you read at the beginning of this story, I am very blessed, and so is my family. Much has been given to us – health, our jobs (no layoffs during COVID), a wonderful community, doing life with our best friends who live next door, and so, so, so much more. Therefore, as a leader in our community, much is expected of me, and I intend to meet that expectation by serving others in need – my staff, their families, and those in our rural communities who have been so greatly impacted by the pandemic.

I want to share a story, one of the many that are heartbreaking, of a family we have been able to serve though this grant. The father is the sole breadwinner in the family and works construction. The mother stays home with their young child, who has an exceedingly rare disability, is immunocompromised, and has significant healthcare needs. Obviously, it is especially important that the father remain employed and stay healthy and keep his family safe. The father's employer failed to inform him when there had been possible exposure to COVID, and his co-workers made fun of him when he wore a mask. They said they did not care if his child had special needs, and they refused to wear PPE around him. Needless to say, the father had to make the tough decision of providing for his family or putting his child's health, and therefore life, at risk due to unsafe environments at work. The father ended up leaving his job and finding a new job in order to keep his family safe.

My agency has been able to help this family with grocery support and paying some of their bills, which has relieved some of the stress of the father during this tough time. Most importantly, we have been able to listen, without judgement, and truly hear what this pandemic has impacted this family and allow them to not only receive but also feel supported and served by our agency.

I leave you with this ... **by serving others, by putting others' needs before mine, by encouraging others**, I think of this verse in Matthew (5:16): "Let your light shine before others, that they may see your good deeds and glorify your Father in heaven." And I take that verse a step further. I hope and pray that others will then decide to "Pay It Forward" and do the same for others and therefore spread the love of our Lord around the globe!

About
Anita Teague

Executive Director
Community Development Center
Shelbyville, TN

Responsible for overseeing and managing the affairs of the agency in accordance with written policies and procedures; works directly with each program manager/director, the administrative staff, and the advisory/governing boards. Serves as a liaison between the agency and the communities served. Fosters the mission of the organization and creates a future vision for the organization including the identification of needed steps to work toward that vision. Responsible for securing financial stability, establishing, and implementing the infrastructure to grow the organization's scope through submission of grants, donations, as well as through corporate and foundation support.

- Utilizes organizational skills to manage and administer the programs of the Community Development Center.

- Maintains oversight as director of programs, reviews, and evaluates the results of program activities, contractual requirements, and program effectiveness.
- Prepares and maintains all contractual correspondence for programs in the Community Development Center.
- Oversees preparation and participates in board meetings, both governing and advisory, committee meetings of the governing board and program meetings as necessary, and serves as a liaison between board and staff.
- Leads staff in identifying short- and long-range plans, policies, and their personal/professional development.
- Represents the agency at state, district, and local levels.
- Utilizing a high degree of concentration, prepares grant proposals, reviews monthly financial statements and reviews

Put Ethics First

By
Dr. Richard L. Baxter

When securing one's first administrative, management appointment, it is natural to have a feeling of euphoria. You quickly envision this being the first step on your road to even greater professional successes. After all, you applied for this position after assuring yourself that you had the intellectual capacity, educational preparation, and consummate skills to tackle the challenges of this new opportunity.

At least that was the mindset with which I entered my first administrative position in higher education as head of the journalism program at Northeast Louisiana University, University of Louisiana Monroe. I was confident in my ability to lead a program that was struggling at the time and therefore gave little thought to the possibility of an ethical conflict derailing my promising career.

In year four of this administrative appointment, I was faced with making a decision that would forever shape my approach to leadership. In addition to my administrative duties, my faculty responsibilities included teaching communication law and advising the student chapter of the Society of Professional Journalists. It was my advisory capacity to the student group that presented the ethical dilemma I would have to navigate.

It was spring semester 1981 when the editor of the student paper and the president of SPJ came to my office and informed me that a group of Student Government Association members was going to try and impeach the SGA president. They had also heard that the SGA was going to close its meeting to the public when the group moved to file the articles of impeachment. The student journalists felt this was a violation of state law, and they wanted to stop this effort for closure. The students wanted to know if I would help them?

Getting involved in a student fight which could get very controversial and embarrassing to the university and outside my primary job responsibilities, I suspected might create problems for me with my superiors. My former wife and I had a pre-kindergarten daughter and had moved to Louisiana from Georgia so that I could take this job. Was I going to put my career at risk, and would my wife agree to me doing so over a disagreement among students?

We convened a meeting of the SPJ chapter at which I asked them if they wanted to take action to block the closure of the SGA meeting. As is often the case with young people, they wanted to storm the barricades regardless of the consequences. It was at that moment that I had wished I had prepared myself for what I would do when faced with an ethical choice that could end my career. In all my planning to become a leader, a situation like this had not been anticipated as part of that preparation.

Since the staff of the student paper were also members of SPJ, I talked to the advisor of the independent paper to see if they were going to take action against the SGA. He told me they would not challenge the closure. This meant I would be going this alone with the students. So, I went to the Dean of Students who advised SGA and asked him if he would work with me to get the SGA leadership to not close the meeting and avoid a confrontation with the journalists. He said that was not his job and politely said I could excuse myself. He would later that day confide that he supported the SPJ students to their president.

On the day of the meeting, SPJ met to discuss its plan for the evening. Having taught communication law, I knew that in the Virginia Newspapers vs. Virginia case, a trial judge had ruled that when reporters initially did not object to him removing the press from the criminal trial the judge had closed, they consented to the closure and therefore waived their right to challenge the action. The U.S. Supreme Court later ruled the press could not be barred from criminal trials except in extraordinary circumstances. In response to the trial judge's ruling, Gannet Newspapers had given all of its reporters a card to read challenging any future government closures before leaving the meeting/trial if they felt it violated state open meetings laws.

Gannett owned the local paper, and I had gotten copies of that card before the SPJ meeting. I told the president of SPJ and the editor of the student paper to rise and read the card when asked to leave the meeting. They were to leave if the SGA refused to continue in open session, but they could set up protest pickets outside the Student Union.

The SGA went from their meeting directly into impeachment proceedings for the president and as expected ordered closure of the trial. Both the paper's editor and the SPJ president read the Gannett card, and we left the meeting.

The trial lasted all night and the student journalists and myself picketed for the duration to protest violation of the state's open meeting law. Since the local media had been banned from the meeting, our protest received plenty of media coverage. Once I had committed to support the students, I never questioned my decision. That episode created a bond with those students that lasted for the next 40 years of my career.

When I went to my office that morning after the protest, a senior executive at the university pulled me inside his office. He told me that while he admired what I was doing, I was being reckless because I was not yet tenured. He warned this could end my job. I thanked him for his concern and left knowing he could be correct.

In reviewing the Louisiana Open Meetings law, I remembered that a local district attorney could bring action against a governmental body which violated the law. My direct supervisor's brother was the district attorney, so I went to my supervisor and asked if he would set up a meeting between me and the district attorney, which he graciously did.

Having always been someone who confronted disagreements directly, I decided I would go see the university president to brief him on my actions and my planned meeting with the district attorney.

The president was gracious enough to see me on immediate notice, but I was anxious as to what his response might be. Was he someone you could trust, and would he appreciate the ethical position I was taking?

I told him that while I hated the embarrassment that this controversy was causing the university, I felt I could not honestly get up in front of students in the future during a communication law class and teach open meetings laws had I not acted when the students asked for help. How could I respond to a student in class who asked why I did nothing when an open meetings violation arose on campus, but still try to teach them about the importance of sunshine laws? I shared with him that I was meeting with the district attorney to see if he felt the SGA violated the law and that the student journalists had agreed to let the district attorney handle it from there. He thanked me for briefing him and said I should do what I felt right.

The district attorney said he had seen the TV coverage of the protests but paid little attention, thinking it was just college students mad at each other. After discussing the details, he said the SGA was a governmental body as a subunit of the university which was a public entity. He called the advisor to the SGA and requested being put on the SGA agenda at its next meeting.

When the meeting convened, the DA informed the SGA members that they had in fact violated the state Open Meetings law by closing their impeachment hearing. He said they had two options. They could either rescind their actions taken at the illegal meeting, or he would file suit against them to negate all actions taken during the meeting. After listening to several SGA members challenge his interpretation, the DA said he was prepared to go to his office and draw up the legal documents that afternoon, and he left. The SGA would vote to void its actions during the contested meeting, the controversy ended, and I would later be granted tenure.

I had dodged the proverbial bullet, but I realized I had been ill prepared to face such a conflict when beginning my leadership position. From that point forward, I began to emphasize that students needed to seriously consider their ethical compass before they joined any organization. What would be the circumstances they would be willing to put their career on the line for their co-workers or subordinates? I told them they could read all the case studies they wanted and have 20-20 hindsight, but they knew they really had nothing on the line when they made those assessments.

Unlike me, they needed to think before becoming a leader what their value system would direct them to do when the consequences of their decision could be life changing? They should ask if their personal ethical norms match those of their profession and their organization. I explained they would be naïve to think they would never face an ethical decision regardless of the organization with which they were associated. The key was understanding what battles you fight and from which you walk away.

After more than 40 years in administration/-

management, I have a substantial number of scars from battles waged. On my last day before retirement, thankfully, I was happy to say that there was never a morning I got up that I could not look in the mirror and feel I had been true to myself. This initial challenge to my personal ethics forged my response to each challenge I encountered in my four-decade career. Put your people's interest ahead of your own. Experience is a great teacher, but mental preparation in advance for ethical issues you may face is equally valuable.

About
Dr. Richard L. Baxter

Dr. Richard L. Baxter's career includes more than 40 years of higher education experience both as a senior executive and as professor of public relations. His appointments have ranged from being the first executive assistant to three university presidents to vice president of university advancement. He was also the first Dean of the College of the Arts at Columbus State University. Prior to his tenure at CSU, he was founding co-owner and publisher of The Business Times of the Rio Grande Valley and co-owner and executive editor of The Business Journal of Corpus Christi in Texas. The Fortune 500, E.W. Scripps Company purchased the publications in 2005.

After reading Dr. Baxter's story about ethics, I was reminded of this verse:

James 2:10 *For whoever keeps the whole law but fails in one point has become guilty of all of it.*

The Leadership Journey
"We trusted your heart"

By
Alan Cole

Leadership invariably has its times of revelation, sometimes referred to as "Ahaa" moments. These moments are not limited to actual real time occurrences. They also may happen in a confluence of experiences that result in a dramatic insight, often triggered by a simple comment, occurrence or thought. In that vein, leaders often see the impact and significance of their efforts reflected in a flash of realization. One might even call this a leadership tipping point, and it may occur well into the leadership journey. In the heat of the leadership battle, many (if not most) true leaders are leading instinctively from a foundation of accumulated experiences and well-honed savvy that can be better understood upon contemplation.

Margaret Thatcher famously quipped **"Being a leader is like being a lady. If you have to remind people you are, you aren't."** Such is the makeup of effective leaders. Theirs is a journey, not defined by events as much as revealed by events. Those times of insights into their own impact and outcomes go well beyond a specific decision or action, but rather accrue in the sum total of such actions. In fact, **leadership is often more recognized by others than by the leader him or herself.** Thus, the need for a leader to declare one's leadership is often a defacto disqualifier to actually being a true leader.

In life, virtually everyone has leadership influence potential, whether realized or not. Likely each of us can think of occasions on which we exhibited strong leadership. And also, likely, we can think of times that our actions were inadequate for the demand(s) of the moment. Leadership is a funny animal. It is even fair to say that like baseball, if you bat .300 or better, you are an all-star. Thousands of wonderful books have been written on leadership, and undoubtably thousands more will be written. As much as we all would love to see leadership defined more explicitly, it remains one of the most qualitative topics of all time. As it is said, I cannot describe it, but I know it when I see it.

One of the most trite questions about leadership is whether leaders are made or born. The consensus answer, according to both research and educated (read that "expert") opinions are BOTH. Some even suggest that leaders are one-third born, and two-thirds made. In that vein, the oft used term "leadership moments" suggests that **leaders emerge in a particular crisis situation, and that somehow in that critical defining moment,** a leader was in fact, born. While true leaders do, in reality, **tend to rise to action in critical scenarios,** the better question is from what foundation do they rise? This foundation is the leadership journey itself, and the resulting leadership trajectory.

In my leadership journey, there have been numerous leadership failures that disappointed me in myself, and yet stiffened my resolve to learn from the failure. General Norman Schwarzkopf of Iraq War fame once stated, **"You learn far more from negative leadership (mistakes) than from positive leadership (success).** Because **you learn how NOT to do it.** And, therefore, **you learn HOW to do it."** It is an inconvenient fact that leaders are forged over time in the crucible of leadership; a lucky few survive to lead on. Many do not.

One of the most poignant "Ahaa" leadership experiences of my 40+ year business career was a particular moment of realization as to the impact that my leadership had on my team, their families, and our community of relationships. Incredibly, I did not fully realize the enormity of this leadership effect until the day we announced my leaving our wonderful team for a promotion to the executive leadership of our parent company. (I will always wonder if that was a wise decision). Here's the story.....

After a season of successful leadership* at Broyhill Furniture, I reluctantly resigned for an opportunity to be an equity partner, in the "turnaround," of a venerable but struggling furniture company in East Tennessee. As only God could orchestrate, I was joining a team of like-minded Christian senior executives in this effort, and we began to lead our business by Biblical principles. Our core philosophy was hiring the best people, pay them well, expect high performance, insist on genuine family/ work balance, and build a culture of respect, and of caring, compassionate relationships.

In short, the results were otherworldly. For almost 10 years, our team became a top performer in our industry: revenue and sales growth were almost 20% per year (CAGR); profitability grew at an astounding 35% annually (CAGR). Our employment grew from 1200 to over 3500, including new plants and capacity maximums in existing plants. The momentum of our success, and the outside perception of our positive culture, created a quiet and confident group of leaders throughout the company. We understood that the sum of our efforts was greater than the parts. That **we were somehow the benefactors of a unique alignment of belief and unity** that multiplied our work geometrically into greater good for our employee families, our community, and our partners. Even as seasoned business leaders we had never experienced this level of total team unity, resulting in sustained quantitative and qualitative success.

Predictably, after the first 5 years of explosive growth, our company was bought by a supportive strategic parent company. And our momentum carried on. Our team had been riding a wave of success for over 8 years. We had a developed a unique chemistry built on a culture of integrity and respect. Our company continued its string of innovative moves, both inside the organization, and in the marketplace. We had a sense of pride and belonging. **We learned to celebrate our wins and turn our losses into lessons, and those lessons into success.** Life was good. (Our team was also growing spiritually, and I never believed that the two were unrelated).

In the midst of this seemingly ever higher ascent, the chairman of our parent company invited me to a rare one-on-one dinner. He was a few years from retirement; I was still in my 40s. After an evening of long discussion, he offered that I move to the corporate office as his eventual successor. For me and my family, this meant coming back to my home state. Being nearer to aging parents. Being closer to our kids' colleges. And a greater business challenge. All the right notes. After weeks of prayer and family discussions, I agreed to accept. And in doing so, I began the decision to determine my successor, and face the task of explaining this decision to our incredible team.......including the reality of closing this chapter of intertwined lives and labor, pride and celebration.

Communication is the oxygen of leadership, and the best communication is face to face. We chose our upcoming quarterly Key Leaders Conference (KLC) for announcing and discussing such a dramatic change of leadership. The KLC, purposely, was not days of endless meetings; it was a celebration of our journey together. We shared our stories, we shared our hits and our strikeouts. We measured our performance and adjusted to the conditions on the ground. We truly became the family that most companies want to be, but few become. And at the end of two days of incredible leadership meetings in spring of 1997, one of our senior executives rose to read the announcement of my leaving to these 50 warriors, because I simply could not do it........

The shock wave of reality was palpable, and deeply emotional. As many openly wept, including and especially me, a line formed with hardly a word spoken. Each warrior, one by one, came forward to hug, to hold, to encourage, and to acknowledge that we would never experience this same chapter again. Maybe other chapters of great merit, but not this one. And in this spontaneous time of farewell, one of our most controversial and contentious executives tearfully expressed words that I will never forget....

"Boss, even when we didn't understand your decisions, we trusted your heart."

If it were possible to distill the essence of leadership into a sentence, this would be it for me. **The flash of realization, my "Ahaa" moment, was that the privilege of leading this team had been concisely expressed in those four words.... "We trusted your heart."** In this decade-long season of highs and lows, wins and losses, laughter and tears, here was the gateway of true leadership: engendering deep and heartfelt TRUST by demonstrating love and respect for those whom we have the privilege of leading by serving. And lest it is not obvious in my words, it was all God's hand of blessing on a team of faithful, diligent followers.

*The term "successful leadership" is a succinct way of expressing the joy and privilege of leading an awesome team at Broyhill Furniture.

About
Alan Cole

Overview

Alan Cole has over 40 years of extensive executive and CEO experience in the home furnishings industry. He recently retired as president of Hooker Furniture Corporation, Martinsville, Va. In this position, Alan was responsible for all operating divisions of Hooker Furniture, and for all U.S. manufacturing operations. Alan also served previously on the Board of Directors of Hooker Furniture, and currently serves on the Board of Directors for Fairfield Chair Company.

Progressive Experience

Alan spent his early professional years developing new and innovative product designs for a variety of furniture manufacturers. In 1983 he became the merchandising and marketing executive for the upholstery division of Broyhill Furniture Industries, one of the largest U.S. manufacturers at that time. In 1985 he was named VP/General Manager of Broyhill Upholstery, which became the largest division of the company.

In 1989, Alan left Broyhill to become a partner and senior executive at The Berkline Corporation, a major manufacturer of motion furniture. In 1991 he became president of Berkline, participating in its sale in 1994 to Masco Corporation. During his tenure, Berkline grew from $75M to $200M+ in sales.

After Berkline's sale to Masco Corporation, Alan was promoted to Executive Vice President of the parent Company, Lifestyle Furnishings International

(LFI), a $2 billion maker of home furnishings with 12 operating divisions, including Henredon, Drexel-Heritage, Lexington, and others. He later became President/CEO of LFI and guided the company through a total divesture in 2001-02. He subsequently joined the board of Hooker Furniture, and later went on to become president of Hooker, until his retirement in 2014. Currently he manages his own executive consulting practice, PARCWest, LLC. based in Winston-Salem, NC.

Accomplishments and Activities

Alan has been blessed with a number of industry awards and honors, including being named Executive of the Year for the US Furniture Manufacturing Industry in 1999, and a Top 25 Furniture Industry Executive in 1994. In 2014 Alan was honored with the Furniture Industry Lifetime Achievement Award by the City of Hope for Cancer Research. He is a charter Board member and former chair of the Furniture Fellowship Board, a Christian industry organization, and a former Board Member of the American Furniture Manufacturers Association. He also serves on the board of the NC Family Policy Council and Troika International.

Alan has served as a speaker and panelist for numerous industry events, and regularly mentors young executives in business ethics and practices. One of Alan's passions is his work with Troika International, a Christian organization that teaches business ethics to business owners and executives primarily in Russia, and Ukraine.

Personal

Alan is married to his wife of 50 years, Patricia (Patti). They have three children (Ryan, Ross, and Carrie) and reside in Winston-Salem, NC. He is a 30+ year runner (one marathon, numerous half marathons), and loves rafting and canoeing. He and Patti have enjoyed teaching young married couples in their churches for over 30 years. He also enjoys traveling internationally in his teaching and mentoring pursuits.

The People

By
Rick Reed

I have been incredibly blessed and fortunate to have served two major aerospace companies as the president and CEO. Over my 43-year career, my experiences have been challenging, intimidating, daunting, and rewarding. There are so many unique stories from year to year that it is difficult, if not impossible, to zero in on one singular experience that stands above all.

What does stand out in the course of my career is that you can **never underestimate the power of your employees, the hands and feet, the hearts, and minds of people.** In fact, I have stated on many occasions that the most important asset of the company's Balance Sheet is the HUMAN resource, the PEOPLE.

This was very evident to me during the last 15 years of my career where I served as president and CEO of a major aerospace company that was involved in designing, certifying, producing, and supporting aircraft systems. Our deliveries were to major producers of aircraft such as Boeing and Airbus.

To demonstrate my own personal way of leading a company and placing high value on the people, let me provide a few examples of the means by which we created a successful company with a work atmosphere that valued its people.

First of all, it was my leadership practice to begin most every workday with a general walk-around company tour. I ventured around the facility through each of the departments, sections and offices talking with employees. I usually talked not only about specific work issues with the employee, but also their own personal areas of family and life. **It was a connection that enabled me to encourage the individual in their work performance and in their struggles with normal life.** I made it a point to reach all levels of the company, from the lowest positions to top management.

Moving beyond a daily "touch" with the workforce, I established a monthly luncheon meeting with employees who were celebrating a birthday in that particular month. These meetings would normally involve about 20 or less of our team members. At these meetings I would usually go around the table and ask each person to share a significant birthday memory. There were always some moments of laughter in this table talk, but we always learned important and key experiences from lives of our fellow workers. During these meetings **I was well known for asking the small group to tell me "what is the dumbest thing we are doing in our company each day."** This question always led to a vibrant discussion but also usually revealed some key weaknesses in the innerworkings and hidden mechanisms of the business.

I incorporated an employee Event and Social Committee and empowered them to develop monthly events that would involve the entire workforce. During the course of our years together, I have indelible memories of different events, including:

- **Chili Cook-Off Competition** - employees brought in their favorite recipe in sufficient quantities that we fed everyone at lunch. The different recipes were numbered, and employees voted on the favorite. Prizes were awarded that included kitchen items and restaurant gift cards.
- **Car and Motorcycle Show** – employees brought in their prized vehicles that were displayed in our parking lot. Once again, we awarded prizes that matched the competition – car wash and wax kits, gift cards to auto stores, etc.
- **March Madness** – the social team always developed an activity that connected to the basketball madness that reaches high levels in our company's region. These would typically include basketball shooting and dribbling contests that involved laughter and prizes. Of course, I would be personally involved and open myself up to well-deserved criticism.
- **Special Pizza and Chick-fil-A luncheons** – we often recognized company financial accomplishments with a Friday lunch and early company shutdown. Reaching the hearts of your people often begins with their stomachs, so it never fails to feed your people. They normally respond with roust work efforts.
- **Annual Summer Picnic** – This was one of the benchmark events and times in the life of my company's focus on the people. We rented an outdoor park facility. The employees cooked turkeys, chicken, hamburgers, and hot dogs. All of our families gathered together, socialized, and

had plenty of fun. Every year the social committee would adopt a theme, e.g. – 50's Hip Hop, Western, Hawaiian, and everyone came dressed according to the theme. This was a never fail, good time event for our people.

•**Annual Christmas Luncheon** – on the Friday before Christmas, our company gathered at a local golf course conference room and experienced the highlight event of the year. This event was always controlled by me, the company president. We always enjoyed a very high-end luncheon meal, but on a few occasions, we switched to an extravagant brunch menu. It was my practice to plan an elaborate program agenda. I would always recognize all new employees that joined our team during the year, and then recognize tenure levels with an envelope with Christmas cash according to the years spent with our company. The program always included a fun video with funny pictures taken throughout the year, including making plenty of fun out of my own self. One year I wrote a Christmas play and had several employees participate as actors. One year we had a talent type of event and had much fun with the program.

It is important to understand that my company had two physical locations, one in North Carolina and one in New York. The practices I mentioned above were mirrored in both locations, with some local variations. For instance, annually we took all of the New York employees on a fishing cruise in Long Island Sound, and we took everyone to a New York

Yankees baseball game. I went back and forth from North Carolina to New York monthly in order to **provide a "ministry of presence"** and to participate in all business and social functions. Needless to say, Delta Airlines and I became fast friends over 15 years, and I was on a first-name basis with many Delta employees.

The point of all of this discussion is to illustrate that my way of leading my company required that I devote plenty of energy to creating a culture that motivated the workforce to "want to be a part of the team." My experience showed me that the **focus on people** produced positive results on our company bottom line. **Our people** always rose to the top in difficult circumstance to deliver 100% Quality/100% On-Time solutions to our customers. I witnessed, numerous times in the life of our company, our employees working into late hours, working weekends, working holidays to deliver our products to our customers. We were never threatened with any form of organizing a union, never lacked in workers raising their hands to take on any challenge. During the course of my 15-year tenure as president, we grew the company from $5M annual revenue to $130M. Our employee roster grew from 35 to 300. We added a 56,000- square-foot engineering center of excellence in order to fully design, develop, and certify aircraft systems. The employees rallied behind all manners of headwinds that we encountered with no reservations. It was joy for me to observe so many individuals achieving success in their workplace.

One final experience that has had far-reaching

impact on my life and career involved a community project with a local elementary school. I had some outside church influence with an elementary school on the edges of our city that has an overwhelming population of underprivileged children in attendance. The principal of that school was desperate for assistance in numerous areas of need and made me aware of the needs. I took this to our company employees and asked if our team had any interest in working together to step in the gap. So, during the course of 3 months, I enabled employees to go to the school during normal working hours and work on the various projects. **The people** of our company pitched in and totally built an outdoor classroom deck, organized multiple storage rooms, and painted a full wall mural in the cafeteria. We concluded our time with a dedication ceremony with the entire school, city dignitaries, and over 100 employees who participated in the work. What an amazing company experience!

In November of 2020, the principal of that school was elected to the North Carolina House of Representatives and she wrote to me saying, "I am forever appreciative of the support you have shown me over the years. As a businessperson, I have sharpened my leadership style by gleaning from you in how much you **led with compassion and focus on your people."**

Bottom line from my experience is that **your people are the key asset in your company**. They are valuable and must be treated with respect and dignity. There will indeed be "problem children" that must be disciplined and held accountable, but this will be more manageable if the **"focus on people"** in the work culture is clearly demonstrated with action.

About
Rick Reed

Rick Reed is the Founder/President and CEO of REED International Aerospace Group, LLC. The company was formed in January 2015 by Mr. Reed, a seasoned aerospace and business executive with 42 years' experience. REED International is dedicated to leveraging and connecting Mr. Reed's extensive technical, operational, and managerial leadership to a broad spectrum of industry. Specific capabilities of REED Intl. include consulting and executive insight that will successfully support the business plans of aerospace / aviation / manufacturing / MRO companies and suppliers around the world.

- Rick is presently leading the Aerospace Economic Development initiative for the Piedmont Triad region, working with the Piedmont Triad Partnership.
- Rick also serves as the Chief Aviation Consultant for Forsyth Technical Community College in their new Aviation Center project at Smith Reynolds Airport in Winston-Salem.
- Since 2016, Rick has served on the Board of NOREGON Systems, Inc.

Richard Reed previously served as President and CEO of Piedmont Aviation Component Services, LLC. The company is a worldwide repair and overhaul service provider for landing gear systems and APU (Auxiliary Power Units) for both commercial and military operators.

From 2000 to 2015, Mr. Reed was President of Triumph Actuation Systems, LLC, in Clemmons, NC, and Freeport, NY. Mr. Reed's position at Triumph included the complete management of the company's design, manufacture, and repair of complex hydraulic and hydro-mechanical aircraft components and systems. The company served a broad, worldwide spectrum of the aviation industry, including commercial airlines and air cargo carriers, original equipment manufacturers of aircraft and aircraft components, and virtually all military applications and platforms.

Prior to joining Triumph, he had been employed with Piedmont Aviation, Inc. for more than 22 years, spending 10 years with Piedmont Airlines in the Maintenance and Engineering Department and then most recently serving as co-owner and Vice President of Aviation Services for Piedmont Aviation Services, Inc., a full-service General Aviation company. Mr. Reed started his aviation career with Boeing Commercial Airplane Company in 1977 as a Flight Controls Engineer.

Mr. Reed completed his undergraduate education at North Carolina State University with a degree in Aerospace Engineering in 1977. He also holds a Commercial pilot's license with Multi-Engine and Instrument ratings. In addition, Reed is an FAA certified Airframe and Powerplant Technician.

In May 2009, Mr. Reed was the Mechanical and Aerospace Engineering Commencement Speaker for North Carolina State University.

In February of 2010, the North Carolina Society of Engineers named Mr. Reed as 2009/2010 Outstanding Engineer of the Year. The award was presented at the 2010 Annual Meeting and Banquet of the Society.

On March 16, 2011, The Rotary Foundation of Rotary International named Rick Reed a Paul Harris Fellow in appreciation of tangible and significant assistance for the furtherance of better understanding and friendly relations among peoples of the world.

On December 15, 2012, at the request of senior United States Senator representing the State of North Carolina, Honorable Richard Burr, the flag of the United States of America was flown over the nation's capital to recognize the induction of Richard Reed into the prestigious North Carolina State University Department of Mechanical and Aerospace Engineering Hall of Fame. His appointment marks his singular professional achievements, outstanding entrepreneurship, and the extraordinary inspiration that he has provided to North Carolina aerospace engineering students. The induction ceremony was held on the Centennial Campus at North Carolina State University on November 1, 2013.

Since 1985 Mr. Reed has served on the Board of Directors of Calvary Baptist Church, including serving as the Chairman the Board. In 2007 Mr. Reed was appointed to serve on the Board of Directors of Troika International. In connection with this, Mr. Reed has taught leadership and business seminars in Amman, Jordan and throughout Ukraine and Crimea. Mr. Reed has also served as Chairman of the Board of Calvary Baptist Day School.

Mr. Reed is married for 42 years, has three daughters, and eight grandchildren.

More information about Mr. Reed can be found on the World Wide Web at: http://www.reedintlaerogroup.com
Twitter@REEDIntlAeroGrp
FACEBOOK – REED International Aerospace Group, L

Wrestling with Success

By
Nikita Koloff

Be prepared. It is better to be prepared for an opportunity and not have one, than have an opportunity and not be prepared.

What led to me becoming a world champion in professional wrestling?

I was not looking for this opportunity, but a door opened and because **I was prepared**, I had success!

My preparation began at the age of 12 when I picked up a magazine called, "Iron Man". It was filled with pictures of bodybuilders, articles about nutrition, and working out. I was hooked. Around that same time, I begin watching the NFL on TV. Once again, I was hooked. I immediately began to crystallize a vision for my life. I would immediately begin working out and exercising to build my body, while at the same time learning the game of football. The goal? Play football in the NFL, followed by a successful coaching career.

Life is filled with setbacks that can hold you back or set you up for a comeback. Subpar grades in high school prevented me from attending a major university. That was a setback, but it did not hold me back. I would enroll in junior college, eventually transferring to a 4-year university and continue my quest for professional football. Two setbacks occurred during my college career, a fractured leg my freshman year and a fractured leg my senior year.

These were setbacks that set me up for a comeback. After graduating college and training for a pro football tryout, a door of opportunity opened up for professional wrestling.

I was not looking to become a professional wrestler, **but I was "prepared" for the opportunity.** With more than a decade of weight training in the gym and several years' experience on the football field, I had paid my dues and was ready for "the call". A five-minute conversation with wrestling promoter Jim Crockett and my career was launched! With no wrestling training, with no experience (amateur or professional), I become a master student and a dedicated lifetime learner.

How can I fail with teachers/mentors like Ivan Koloff, Don Kernodle, Dusty Rhodes, Ric Flair, Ricky Steamboat, Johnny Weaver and so many more? All in all, **I have never considered myself a student greater than the teacher. We all need mentors, someone who can teach us, train us, and disciple us. Mentors are role models, someone you admire, a person you respect, someone who inspires and someone who provides, a Guiding Light.**

What led to my quick rise to stardom? **The 3 D's. Desire, dedication, and discipline.** I had the desire to succeed, I was dedicated to making it happen, and I disciplined myself all along the way. It was a mindset. A great quote from Oliver Wendell Holmes says, "Man's mind stretched to a new idea never goes back to its original dimension." I was gaining the knowledge, but I also had to combine that with talent. I clearly had the talent but always remember this, **talent can take**

you to the top, but character will sustain you. A great quote from Dwight L. Moody says, "You take care of your character, your reputation will take care of itself." **Character is a gift you give yourself.**

Change the world by changing you. Ready for the secret to success? Success is not instant, it is consistent! If you desire to be more successful, shift from excuse thinking to creative thinking. **Change the way you think, so you can change the way you act, so you can change your outcome. You determine how you think, you determine how you act, and you determine your outcomes.**

Here is a truth. You have been "wrestling" your whole life, wrestling with your time, money, family, priorities, decisions, and opportunities. The lesson is this: **Most people spend more time wrestling with the problem then wrestling with the solution.** The objective is to pin down the answer, to find the solution. **The only defeat you will ever incur is when you quit.** Be one who concentrates on a solution and you will have a better outcome.

In conclusion, every man or woman is limited by three things:

- The knowledge in his or her mind
- The strength of his or her character
- The principles upon which he or she is building his or her life

The best measure of success and fulfilment is to compare what you have done to your true potential. Are you living up to your potential? Here is a great quote from John Ruskin, "The first test of a really great man (or woman) is their humility." **No matter how successful you become, remain humble.**

About
Nikita Koloff

Nikita Koloff/Koloff for Christ Ministry http://www.nikitakoloff.com/ for 27 years, traveled all 50 states, 30 countries; host of "It's Time To Man Up" Podcast & Broadcast on Truth Radio Network; facilitated 50+ men's camps; conduct Man Up conferences; ministered in 1200+ churches; preach crusades, revivals, church services; have four daughters, Teryn, Tawni, Kendra, Kolby, nine grandchildren; and enjoy weightlifting, playing golf, watching college football.

Reluctant Learning and Leading

"Teachers have three loves: love of learning, love of learners, and the love of bringing the first two loves together" Scott Hayden

By
Martha Lennon

This story begins in a mid-1950s classroom with five children sitting in small chairs in front of a teacher. This was the most dreaded time of the day when a little girl tried to make sense of the pictures and print in the book she held with sweaty palms. This little group certainly had a name like the other small groups that proceeded, but for this learner, the group name was buzzards, and she was a reluctant learner. Fast forward twelve years when the time came for college major decisions. Since this learner never excelled in math, science or languages, the choice of a college major was limited. Education was a good idea, advised her mother who had in her early years been a teacher.

So, the future is set not out of passion but by default. After all the teacher preparations, marriage, travel and family became my classroom for many years.

Why are you reading this introduction? **God can use anyone for His purposes,** but He chose to put me on a pathway for learning, teaching others, and eventually into leadership positions turning into a 35-year career in education. In reflection, I assumed that I was just taking care of family financial needs although with some reluctance, but God had a road for me to travel. His first assignment was to teach and lead in a church weekday education program for five years.

On a whim, an application was submitted to teach in the public schools. Much to my surprise, I was hired and assigned to a school. As the principal was walking me around the building, he asked me what my professional goals were. Here I was just doing the next thing, and I responded that I would like to spend a couple of years in the classroom before moving to administration. As I sat in my empty classroom, I wondered where that thought originated since I had never been one to set long-term goals. Seeing something in me that I did not see in myself, the school leadership team placed me in positions of leadership in the school beyond the classroom. District leadership took me under leadership wings and provided additional training and opportunities to lead locally and at the state level.

Teaching and leading brought a great deal of joy, but a career move for my husband offered a new season of life where my position was not needed for our family's financial needs. I packed up the classroom with reluctance thinking that my teaching years were behind me.

Speaking through the prophet Jeremiah, God told His people that He knew the plans that He had for them, and those plans were good and would give a future and a hope. (Jeremiah 29:11) God had more plans for this reluctant learner, and the plans were beyond imagination. For the next 22 years, God provided an incredible learning community for me to grow professionally, and to learn extensively to lead a cadre of highly dedicated, professional, Christian teachers. As with other seasons of life, God led me to step out in faith for His next. During that first year of what some call retirement, I slept, prayed, and turned to Scripture to seek God's face for this next season of life. **To help keep life in perspective, I purchased a ¼ cup measuring cup to place by my kitchen window as a reminder; I had only about ¼ of my life remaining to pour out into the lives of others and thus began a new season of learning, teaching, and leading.**

God in His faithfulness led me to identify two passions, and they both required learning and leading. The first passions was to know God through His Word. Not just the Sunday School stories but to dig deep into the Old Testament to understand the nature and character of the holy God. The old saying, "once a teacher, always a teacher" kicked in, and I began to teach other women how to study the Bible using inductive study skills as I was also learning. I began this new passion by becoming a reluctant student sitting under the instruction of Precept Ministries. I say reluctant because in the back of my mind, I remembered that small reading circle and the struggle to make sense of the printed page. Now a decade later, that passion has provided an entirely new place of learning and leading outside the traditional school walls.

The second passion God revealed to my heart was the desire to invest in the lives of younger women. Mentoring is the new buzzword for being a friend.

Since my children were very young, I asked God to provide other adults to join me in influencing and loving my children, knowing that I could not always be physically close for those intimate chats. I assumed that I would put the word out that I wanted to meet some younger women and then start a book study or Bible study with another small group, but God had so much to teach me about His Ways. But God had another plan and "but God" has become one of my favorite phrases from Scripture.

I was sitting in a large women's ministry gathering and I focused on the speaker. There was a young woman in my direct line of sight. I realized that I had been in another setting with her where I heard her speak from her heart with passion and some deep hurt. The leader from the meeting even suggested that I might want to reach out to her. Now here she was in my line of sight for an hour. At the conclusion of the morning session, I walked over to her table, put my personal card with my name and contact information down in front of her saying if she ever wanted to talk, give me a call. She looked up at me with wide eyes that quickly filled with tears and said that she had asked God for an older woman to spend time sharing with. I had not expected that response and stammered out, "Give me a call." Another season of teaching and leading began.

God is teaching me that women of all ages want community, and He has brought women of diverse ages into my life. There have been times when we met weekly with interval phone and text messages to walk through a crisis. Other times, it is a monthly coffee break or lunch outing. I admit that sometimes I am reluctant when the time for our meetings come. Those feelings of inadequacies, not being smart enough, come rushing into the mind. But God just wants me available to walk through life with these women, teaching and leading as I offer up my mistakes and small victories as signs of hope of God's faithfulness.

But God had more for me. He took the two passions, **teaching** the Word and **mentoring** younger women across the world to Lviv, Ukraine. How I got there is a story for another time, but in this later season of life God provided a ministry with young women enrolled in the Ukrainian Baptist Theological Seminary as I lead and teach them how to **know God through Scripture and how to mentor other women**.

As a new teacher, I did not know that I would learn to love teaching, but now I understand that God placed that in my DNA in my mother's womb. Only a sovereign God could take a reluctant learner and place her in the field of education. I did not know that I would so deeply **love the learners** that He places in my pathways, but I do know that there is nothing sweeter in life than teaching and leading other women in their spiritual journey. God took this reluctant learner and showed her the great adventure of following Him.

About
Martha Lennon

Education
- Meredith College – BA in Sociology and Education
- Old Dominion University – MsEd – Education
- UNCG – MsEd in Educational Leadership (licensure program)
- UNCG – Post Doctoral studies in Educational Leadership with a focus on women in leadership

Work Experience
- 30+ years in field of education
- 27 years in Christian education
- 22 years as Head of School for Calvary Day School
- Executive Educational Consulting Services (coaching service)
- Retired in 2008

Community Involvement:
- Bible Fellowship Teacher – Calvary Church
- Precept Inductive Bible Study Leader – Calvary Church
- Volunteer in Calvary Assimilation/Membership offices
- Military Officers Association of America
- Forsyth County Nursing Home Advisory Committee
- PEO – Organization that supports the educational pursuits of women
- DAR

Serves on multiple scholarship selection committees

Passions and Hobbies:
- Teaching women how to study the Bible.
- Currently leading three Zoom classes each week with over 50 women enrolled
- Mentoring younger women both spiritually and professionally
- Reading (I love to read historical fiction); knitting (I knit baby blankets for newborns at our local hospital)
- Crocheting
- Needlepoint

Personal
- Married for 52 years to Dennis Lennon
- 2 adult children; 5 grandchildren

Leaders Do Not see problems.
They See Opportunities.

By
Tom Burklow

In today's environment we have created a flawed and impossible definition, or idea, of what makes a leader. This has progressed to a point where we have created a self-fulfilling prophecy of failure for those who are willing to step into the role. The current expectation of a leader is one of no room for error, mistakes, or risk taking. They are expected to have flawless execution of those decisions. The byproduct of this is an environment where those who have a valuable role to play in our society, step back or turn away from a role they are well suited for. Included in this misconception is the symbolism of past leaders. Take your pick, Lincoln, Patton, Kennedy, Martin Luther King. You do not have to see your role as similar to theirs to be a valued leader. We are missing leaders in many areas of our society. Families need leaders. Young people need leaders. You do not need to move mountains to provide leadership. You need to be there and be willing to step up.

When teaching entrepreneurship to high school students a common trait I see is fear. Fear of failure, fear of making mistakes, and the fear of how they will be looked upon for not being perfect. It is a fear of risk taking. Let's look at fear and risks. Young people will drink and drive, text and drive, drive over the speed limit, and not see that as being too risky. However, ask a classroom full of them a question, or to propose a solution, and there is silence and avoidance. They fear being wrong and not having the "right" answer. It is not a reach to understand this, as states and other educational influencers push standardized tests and assessments on students where knowing the "right" answer matters. Students have the consequences of not having the "right" answer etched into their brains at a very early age.

In class, we have many discussions about what failure really is. Failure is eliminating possibilities while working your way to a solution. The only real failure is not taking the time to look at a less than optimum outcome, analyze the results objectively, and move forward. The motto in class is, "Even a bad plan is better than no plan." This is not a new concept, but it is important to recognize this process as normal. Without a plan an endpoint cannot be identified. Without an endpoint identified there is no direction. The only component that must be identified is that the plan is fluid, a living process that identifies obstacles which then guides the plan to the next way point while focusing on the endpoint. In vehicle rider education we teach, you go where you look even if that is not where you want to go. This ties in directly with the importance of having a plan to give you focus on where you want to go. Each obstacle identified requires you to look where you want to go as you move to the next, more refined, step in the solution.

In class, we look at the failures of some of the world's most successful entrepreneurs. These entrepreneurs are often flawed in significant ways. Often it is an extremely bad life event, or personal flaw, that brought their leadership skills to the front. They had skill sets they had either not recognized, or they had suppressed for fear of failure until a problem presented itself. On the topic of problems, **leaders do not see problems, they see opportunities.** Opportunities to improve a situation temporarily, or in the long term.

I have made many of the mistakes listed above. **As a leader in my classroom, I share my mistakes** openly, I own them and share my "take away" from those experiences. A leader must role model ownership and honesty.

Part of leadership is to accept that, to some person or group, you are seen as a role model even if you don't want to be one. It is at this point, I refer them to one of my earlier lessons in life. That lesson was, **"To not decide, is to decide."** Just because you decide not to decide, the events around you will not stop as a result of your lack of decision making. Something is still going to happen. **This means you have chosen to be a passenger and not the rudder.** Young people often think by not participating in a discussion they are safe from making a mistake, when in reality they just made the most commonly repeated and potentially costly mistake. This was true in my life also.

Throughout high school, college, and those years after college I took the safe choices for fear of failing and looking bad. Yet, in my life post college I gave no thought to riding my motorcycles in all conditions, coast to coast and in competition well into triple digit speeds. June 20th, 1983 at 11:15am my life moment came.

I was running the sales end of a large motorcycle dealership and assisting with strategic planning and being a general jack of all trades. That was still a safe zone, as I didn't know what I didn't know, but I knew the product and the market as well as anyone else. I had worked in this shop during college and I would consider the primary owner a friend on a professional level. The mail arrived, and shortly after the owner dropped by to make sure we were all earning our pay. I mentioned to him he had a package in the other office. He returned to the office tugging on the heavily taped package within a couple of feet of myself and a young salesman. He wandered out of the office to get a box cutter. Little did I know that a box with a mousetrap, a 9 volt battery, blasting cap ,and three railroad torpedoes had just walked out of the room. Seconds later a noise shook the building to its foundation. As I looked up, I saw my salesman duck and look to the right as debris flew in all directions. From there it was like it is often described, things went into slow motion. Seconds felt like minutes, and you noticed incredible detail to every event with your eyes, ears and nose.

After exiting the building, I turned and looked back in the door with dark smoke lofting across the ceiling. I went back into the building and headed towards the location of the explosion. I remember pausing for what seemed like forever at the edge of the showroom looking into a smoke-filled parts department scattered with debris. I heard a groaning noise and more items falling and moving. I thought, should I go there and help? I stopped and pondered what I may encounter and what mark it might leave on me, then I went into the smokey darkness.

In the dim light I found a person, whoses injuries were severe and not encouraging. Every step of the way there was an opportunity to turn back and take the safe option. I didn't. As it turns out the person was my employer and friend. Life for me arrived at a pivot point. Not because of the loss of his life, but because of the event. That was my "moment". Almost to a second I can identify a change in my view of decision making and risk taking. Fear of failure almost vanished immediately. That day brought the realization to me that sitting on the **sidelines, avoiding risk and failure, does not stop life from happening.**

Chaos ensued for the next several months. The business' vision and direction vanished. The few days I was away from the business, while the investigation proceeded, my mind began to click into stepping up and facing some facts. It was peak season, we had twelve families that needed a paycheck, and we had talent on tap. No announcements were made. We just went back to doing what we do. I can't say that I, or any of us, announced ourselves as the leader. At Age 25, I was finally going to wade into the leadership pool.

Each morning began with me crawling around under my car, carefully opening doors and the hood ,looking for foreign devices. Probably driven by a bit of anger, I set about making decisions. I learned to ask for forgiveness, not permission. I put all of the communication skills I had learned in college and sales training to work with "the crew". Every day saw any number of opportunities to learn about being a leader, though I didn't recognize that was what I was doing. We fought through countless obstacles on top of running a small business for the next 5 years. Eventually, the economy in the industry became too much to survive. The new owners asked what my thoughts were for moving forward with the two stores. My outline didn't include me. They were puzzled by this. My reply was, they asked what I would suggest regarding the business's survival, not my wants or needs. **Leaders do not prioritize themselves.**

I stepped away from the industry for a while. Only then was I able to look at those five years from the outside and take an inventory of what had transpired. I had lost my temper many times, handled personnel issues poorly, but I had sharpened my personal organization and time management skills. I learned to make decisions based on what I knew at the moment and move on. One must also look back and reflect honestly with the outcome and how they could have been done better.

I also took stock of the assets I had to work with, great people. **A leader needs to be observant of the people they are working with and know them.** I learned that not knowing and learning to seek advice, was not a weakness, but was part of being a leader. Did I single handedly do this, not at all. I would estimate for every success I had, there were three missteps. Over the next thirty plus years I found the definition of leadership as it applied to me. It is a willingness to step up when needed, regardless of the role. We all have this ability within us.

You are already that leader. You are that leader that will influence the lives of a group of young people who will then take that experience forward and create success in many others. You are that leader who will be a role model for a young person seeking answers about growing into a leader for their family and their community. Those leaders scattered across our communities are playing an ongoing role every day that will impact generations.

Guidelines for being a leader
•To not decide, is to decide to be afraid
•Learn to adapt and teach how to adapt
•Lead by example, not by intimidation
•Honor your mistakes by learning from them

About
Tom Burklow

Mr. Burklow is an educator with 23 years of experience at the high school, adult education, and college level. He is the recipient of the Weaver Oratory award (Eastern Kentucky University) and the Donna Petrocy Monroe Local Schools Educator of the Year Award (2008).

His core subject areas are Web Design, Accounting, Business Communications and Entrepreneurship. He has also taught Business Law, Introduction to Business, Economics, Digital Video Production, Speech-Information, and Technology.

Mr. Burklow has also produced a student directed and managed historical documentary covering the 123-year history of the Lemon-Monroe School District. This project also included archiving and digitizing local history and oral histories for the community.

Prior to his work as an educator Mr. Burklow worked in the PowerSports Industry for 20+ years in the Service, Retail sales, leadership areas, along with Industry trade organizations, manufacturers, and as a consultant to the Japanese motorcycle OEDs. Burklow also co-founded the international motorcycle exchange company, Trans-Atlantic BikeShare Worldwide. (1992-2006)

Mr. Burklow holds a B.A. in Mass Communications with a business minor (Eastern Kentucky University) and a B.A. in Secondary - Business Comprehensive Education (Wright State University, Magna Cum Laude)

CHAPTER FOUR

In these Times

You have now come to the completion of a journey involving our history as a nation, the many opportunities and skills, suggestions, and opportunities to learn about teaching and leading in the family and at work. You have also been given lessons from other leaders as guideposts and opportunities to discover how to lead in your faith. 2020 and 2021 will be one of those years in the life of our nation that will be recorded in history as momentous. You still have a role to play in its making. I pray that you will be guided in a Christian way as we continue to heal our nation. In this closing Chapter I will share with you three important steps to help all of us toward revival for our nation. These three steps are: Where are we now? Where do we need to go? And What can I do?

Just turn on the TV or read the news: injustice, evil, and terrible influences are all around us. Christians in America are crying out, families are crying out, those that are sworn to protect us are crying out. Let's be clear about my view, and that is we are all the same race in humanity. Color does not matter, where you live does not matter, what language you speak does not matter. We are all God's children. America is crying out, just as in ancient times when Habakkuk cried out to God. We must be optimistic that God's plan is working and will be resolved in His timing. We can still cry out to God, and we can pray for intervention. Trust must be in Him.

Recently in my Bible fellowship class our teacher, Jack Bales, introduced us to some eye-opening situations taking place now. Jack shared with us an article by Jan Markell titled "Suddenly – In the Twinkling of An Eye" from the Olive Tree Ministries. As you read the following, what a wake-up call this is for us in these times. I quote Jan Markell as she said:

•"Our fairly ordinary world suddenly vanished. Stores sold out suddenly.
•Fear gripped America – and the world suddenly.
•People were ordered to change their lifestyles suddenly, totally.
•People lost businesses of a lifetime suddenly.
•A U.S. president went from popular to "the cause of it all" suddenly.
•Reality became surreal suddenly.
•Cities turned into ghost towns suddenly.
•Mankind became lovers of self, treacherous, and without self-control suddenly.
•Cries for global government transpired suddenly, as if a one-world system could slow down the wreckage.
•Virtual became the new way of doing all things suddenly.
•The U.S. economy went from best ever to horrible suddenly.
•Church went from essential to irrelevant in the eyes of the world suddenly.
•Hollywood suddenly stopped making sick movies as theaters suddenly closed.
•Order turned to chaos suddenly with racial tension.
•That tension suddenly turned to lawlessness.
•Lawlessness turned to anarchy suddenly.
•The cry for police protection suddenly turned to 'abolish the police.'
•Common sense simply turned suddenly to "strong delusion".

Now is the time that Christians in America must suddenly wake up. Now is that time that our churches must suddenly wake up. Now is the time that we must suddenly spread God's word as never before. Now in the time we must suddenly begin to heal our nation. Now is the time for us to suddenly become one that is an instrument of change. I pray that we are ready. Others are suddenly, as never before, beginning to pray all across our nation.

If you think that these sudden changes are alarming, take a look at this. One day I received an email from a friend in my Bible fellowship class. In this email he was sharing a letter that came from an anonymous source with no author mentioned. Well, I did a little research and was able to find out who pinned the article. It was written by William Draughon (at Common Sense for The Common Man). I reached out to William and asked his permission to quote him in this book. He agreed. His words ring loud and true in these times, and I quote him.

"I never dreamed that I would have to face the prospect of not living in the United States of America, at least not the one I have known all my life. I have never wished to live anywhere else. This is my home, and I was privileged to be born here.

But today I woke up, and as I had my morning coffee, I realized that everything is about to change. No matter how I vote, no matter what I say, something evil has invaded our nation, and our lives are never going to be the same.

I have been confused by the hostility of family

and friends. I look at people I have known all my life – so hate-filled that they agree with opinions they would never express as their own. I think that I may well have entered the Twilight Zone.

You cannot justify this insanity. We have become a nation that has lost its collective mind!

- If a guy pretends to be a woman, you are required to pretend with him.
- Somehow, it is un-American for the census to count how many Americans are in America.
- Russians influencing our elections are bad, but illegals voting in our elections are good.
- It was cool for Joe Biden to "blackmail" the president of Ukraine, but it is an impeachable offense if Donald Trump inquiries about it.
- Twenty is too young to drink a beer, but eighteen is old enough to vote.
- People who have never owned slaves should pay slavery reparations to people who have never been slaves.
- People who have never been to college should pay the debts of college students who took out huge loans for their degrees.
- Immigrants with tuberculosis and polio are welcome, but you'd better be able to prove your dog is vaccinated.
- Irish doctors and German engineers who want to immigrate to the U.S. must go through a rigorous vetting process, but any illiterate gangbangers who jump the southern fence are welcome.

•$5 billion for border security is too expensive, but $1.5 trillion for "free" healthcare is not.
•If you cheat to get into college you go to prison, but if you cheat to get into the country you go to college for free.
•People who say there is no such thing as gender are demanding a female president.
•We see other countries going Socialist and collapsing, but it seems like a great plan to us.
•Some people are held responsible for things that happened before they were born, and other people are not held responsible for what they are doing right now.
•Criminals are caught and released to hurt more people but stopping them is bad because it's a violation of THEIR rights.
•And pointing out all this hypocrisy somehow makes us "racists"?!"

Nothing makes sense anymore, no values, no morals, no civility, and people are dying of a Chinese virus, but it's racist to refer to it as Chinese, even though it began in China. We are clearly living in an upside down world where right is wrong and wrong is right, where moral is immoral and immoral is moral, where good is evil and evil is good, where killing murderers is wrong, but killing innocent babies is right.

Wake up America, the great unsinkable ship Titanic America has hit an iceberg, is taking on water, and is sinking fast. The choice is yours to make. What will it be? Time is short, make your choice wisely!"

William Draughon could not be clearer.

As you know, an amazing event took place on September 26, 2020. Tens of thousands of Christians gathered at our nation's capital to pray for repentance and revelation for our nation. I have never seen anything like this before. Not only did this take place at our capital but also in other cities across our great nation; thousands and thousands of people praying for healing in cities around the world! For such a time as this, millions of prayers were lifted up that day, before that day, and since that day. Prayers for revival, prayers for peace and restoration. I will never forget that day.

So, I say to you that life is not a bed of roses, but we can surely watch out for those thorns that can prick us in our life. Remember that there is a Glorious End and Beginning coming one day. Let us avoid the thorns of life and help others. Some of those thorns are best described in the following scriptures:

II Timothy 3:1-5 NKJV
But know this, that in the last days perilous times will come: For men will be lovers of themselves, lovers of money, boasters, proud, blasphemers, disobedient to parents, unthankful, unholy, unloving, unforgiving, slanderers, without self-control, brutal, despisers of good, traitors, headstrong, haughty, lovers of pleasure rather than lovers

of God, having a form of godliness but denying its power.
And from such people turn away!

1 John 2:15-17 KJV

Love not the world, neither the things that are in the
world. If any man love the world, the love of the Father is
not in him. For all that is in the world, the lust of the flesh,
and the lust of the eyes, and the pride of life, is not of the
Father, but is of the world. And the world passeth away,
and the lust thereof: but he that doeth the will of God
abideth forever.

Now that you know about the thorns, when
advised to turn away, the implication is to not be led
into the vine that you, too, will become a thorn. If
you do encounter a thorn, you have an opportunity,
and I would say an obligation, to witness to a person
or a group the salvation Christ provides. You just
might pluck that thorn right off of the vine.

Where are we now? Again, we must revisit
truth. In today's world there is much false teaching
taking place in churches, in education, and in
politics. Many are not speaking the truth but rather
building themselves up for their own gratifications.
As Christians, we must stand up for truth and be
strong in our faith. Be sure you are satisfied that the
truth is being communicated.

Isn't it terrible that in the news much information
is taken out of context, and that we now need to
have fact checkers in the news and on social media
to verify context? Whatever happened to the plain
old news where the facts were presented, and we got

to decide our viewpoint. Now the news is trying to fashion what our views should be.

Leviticus 19:18 NIV
Do not seek revenge or bear a grudge against anyone among your people, but love your neighbor as yourself.

Beyond just the news in these times, there are many who do not respect the authority of those that protect us. Therefore, whoever resists the authorities resists what God has appointed, and those who resist will incur judgement. Look at the many protests that have taken place in 2020. The leaders that are not protecting our rights and liberties are a terror of evil conduct. "We all then should do what is good, and you will receive his approval, for he is God's servant for your good. But if you do wrong, be afraid, for he does not bear the sword in vain. For he is the servant of God, an avenger who carries out God's wrath on the wrongdoer." This should be a warning to those who defy the law. Justice will prevail at some time, and victory will be the truth, and those who have broken our laws and His, will one day be held accountable. Just remember these verses:

1 John 3:4
Everyone who makes a practice of sinning also practices lawlessness; sin is lawlessness.

Proverbs 6:16-19 ESV

There are six things that the Lord hates, seven that are an abomination to him: haughty eyes, a lying tongue, and hands that shed innocent blood, a heart that devises wicked plans, feet that make haste to run to evil, a false witness who breathes out lies, and one who sows discord among brothers.

Matthew 24:12-14

And because lawlessness will be increased, the love of many will grow cold. But the one who endures to the end will be saved. And this gospel of the kingdom will be proclaimed throughout the whole world as a testimony to all nations, and then the end will come.

Amos 5:12

For I know how many are your transgressions and how great are your sins — you who afflict the righteous, who take a bribe, and turn aside the needy in the gate.

As an architect, I understand the importance of a well-designed foundation. However, I have seen things that have been destroying a structural foundation. In America today, the foundations of our heritage and belief are being eaten away by; Sin, Abortion, Antifa, Lawlessness, and Socialism. The illustration on the next page represents this:

To help heal our nation we must return to the values that our nation was founded on. We cannot be a nation for everything. If we are for everything then what will govern us? We will no longer be able to say the Pledge of Allegiance, which has already been removed from many of our schools and government entities. Let us never forget!

"I pledge allegiance to the Flag ... and to the Republic for which it stands, one Nation under God, indivisible, with liberty and justice for all."

Where do we need to go?

In life it is extremely important to know where you are and what is happening around you. If you want to succeed, you then need to determine where you need to go. This is a turning point for our nation this year. I have to be honest and say that we should all pray for God's perfect will this year and in our future.

Franklin Graham actually said it better than me: "We need a Christian revolution in America. Let's support men and women at every level of government – at local, state, and national – who will lead this country back to really being one nation under God, so that we can truthfully say, once again, "In God we trust.""

In his recent book "Saving a Sick America", Michael Brown shares a deep and fervent hope that another great awakening (a revival) could be at hand, something that could rock our nation from coast to coast. It is not too late for America!

We need to go to Him.

II Timothy 2:24-26

And the Lord's servant must not be quarrelsome but kind to everyone, able to teach, patiently enduring evil, correcting his opponents with gentleness. God may perhaps grant them repentance leading to a knowledge of the truth, and they may come to their senses and escape from the snare of the devil, after being captured by him to do his will.

The Greek word for "repentance" is "metanoia," and it's not just remorse or regret, but it means "a change of mind." So, revival cannot occur until there has first been a change of mind, and this takes the Spirit of God, and only God can grant repentance.

We need to go to Him.

Psalm 46:1-2
God is our refuge and strength, a very present help in time of trouble. Therefore, we will not fear...

We must not be fearful in these times. Because of COVID-19, I see so many people fearful of getting close to another person when I am out and about. I have friends that have high anxiety about wearing masks. I know people that are fearful of going out at night because they think the road might be blocked by protesters (those that break the law). We must not be fearful; we must be calm. We must be secure in Him. Then we can withstand the forces of evil.

Psalm 46:
This psalm expresses thanks for the deliverance of Jerusalem, "the city of God" (verse 4). It contains three key ideas. First, God is a place of security when all else is insecure (verses 1-3). Second, God protects His city, giving its people assurance and comfort (verses 4-7). Third, all men are called upon to consider God's works and submit to His authority (verses 8-11).

Remember **Psalm 18:2**
The Lord is my rock, my fortress and my deliverer; my God is my rock, in whom I take refuge. He is my shield and the horn of my salvation, my stronghold.

Matthew 11:28-30

"Come to me, all you who are weary and burdened, and I will give you rest. Take my yoke upon you and learn from me, for I am gentle and humble in heart, and you will find rest for your souls. For my yoke is easy and my burden is light."

If this book should reach the hands of someone who is aborting children, assuming identities other than what God created us to be, destroying others' property, setting fires that destroy livelihoods, I pray that you will lay your burdens down as illustrated in the following image. Then seek repentance and forgiveness and never harm others again but have a mission to help others.

Image of "Lay your burdens down"

As a parent, do you know what your children are doing.? If you don't, then it is time for you to show the leadership, you have been entrusted. Reach out to them, talk with them, pray for them before their sinful actions upon our nation locks them up. I do not know of a single parent that wants their children incarcerated. It is never too late for you to act. You can save a life. You can prevent harm from coming to another. You can help to heal our nation.

If you are protesting against our nation, lay your burdens down. Walk away from a destructive lifestyle that harms others and perpetuates your sinful action. Stop now, and return to Him.

We need to go to Him.

As we begin to heal our nation, we need to:

- Bring healing to those that injustice has harmed.
- Bring more Christians into national, state, and local governments.
- Bring the pledge of allegiance back to our schools and, do not take the word God out of the pledge.
- Bring prayer back into everything.
- Bring Christ back into our education.
- Bring friends into the fellowship of believers.
- Bring an end to lawlessness.
- Bring an end to killing.

The Christian citizens of America can bring about a saving and healing change to our nation. Now is not the time to be silent, now is the time to stand up and be heard. Now is the time to be brave. Now is the time to be active in our school system, local, state, and national government. Now is the time for our churches to do the same thing and not be fearful of the reactions of others. Pastors must lead from the pulpit from God's words and not the words of the community.

What can I do?

Pray

As Americans, now is the time to ask ourselves, "What can I do to help others heal our nation? What must we do to help others heal our nation? What must we do to keep America Great?" We can start by being thankful in all. Before the sun sets today, stop and take some time to think about what you are thankful for. It might your family, your job, your faith, maybe even your life. Prayer should reveal thankfulness. Prayer is so important as we communicate with God, through Jesus Christ.

Illustration from the book:
Route 66-Have you found your route in life?

I JOHN

From this illustration above we must help bring others from their darkness into His light if we are to heal our nation.

Philippians 2:14-15

Do all things without murmurings and disputings: 15 That ye may be blameless and harmless, the sons of God, without rebuke, in the midst of a crooked and perverse nation, among whom ye shine as lights in the world.

Remember, as I have mentioned earlier, that we never know who is watching us. Let all who look at us see us as a shining light, causing them to seek the knowledge of what makes us appear in this manner. I remember a time that I was in a former communist country, and I was approached by someone that had been observing me for a while. I was asked, "Why are you always smiling and seem happy?" My response was, "Because I have the love of Christ in my heart." The person then wanted to know more about me.

We must be examples!

I cannot begin to imagine how Paul's life as a warrior in prayer, affected others; his thanksgivings in hardships; his love and prayers for other saints (believers), bishops, and churches ! We are never too young or too old to pray. But prayer should be a part of our daily life. Paul is just one example which I chose to illustrate while he was in prison in Rome. If you have not prayed today, I hope you will before the sun sets. God knows your heart, so communicate with Him. Let us shine as lights in the world.

2 Chronicles 7:14 KJV

"If my people, which are called by my name, shall humble themselves, and pray, and seek my face, and turn from their wicked ways; then will I hear from heaven, and will forgive their sin, and will heal their land." We must be examples!

Read your Bible.

If we merely study the Word of God, and do not put it into practice, then faith is nothing more than an intellectual exercise. The Bible is the most read book in the world, an incredible source of wisdom, truth, teaching and leadership. Can you imagine what the world would be like if we could be leaders and teachers like Christ. There are many people of faith who try to, but that is the best we can do. We are not perfect.

1 Timothy 4:13 ESV
Until I come, devote yourself to the public reading of Scripture, to exhortation, to teaching.

In my city there is a local group of Christian men who meet weekly to share their testimonies, conduct prayer walks in the city, and support each other as brothers in Christ. This organization is "The New Canaan Society." Every Friday before 7:00 AM, men volunteer to participate in the public reading of the scripture.

2 Timothy 3:16
All Scripture is breathed out by God and profitable for teaching, for reproof, for correction, and for training in righteousness.

Read your Bible! Do not say God is silent when your Bible is closed.

Psalm 119:105
Your word is a lamp to my feet and a light to my path.

Of course, there is that book of Proverbs. What an amazing book to read and teach and lead our young and ourselves. It's timeless and covers many areas of life such as anger, children, education, law, marriage, work ... just to mention a few. I wish that these wisdoms could appear more in our educational systems for life preparations for our children. Please find a Bible and read Proverbs. Use this knowledge for yourself, but more importantly share these wisdoms with others so they will be on the right route in life so our nation can heal. Here is what others have said about this:

- **Charles Spurgeon** was quoted as saying:
  "Nobody ever outgrows Scripture; the book widens and deepens with our years."
- **Helen Keller.** Someone who could not see, but could see things in ways I cannot imagine:
  "Unless we form the habit of going to the Bible in bright moments as well as in trouble, we cannot fully respond to its consolations because we lack equilibrium between light and darkness."
- **Mark Twain** had this to say about reading the Bible:
  "Most people are bothered by those passages of Scripture they do not understand, but the passages that bother me are those I do understand."
- **John Quincy Adams:** "So great is my veneration for the Bible, that the earlier my children begin to read it, the more confident will be my hopes that they will prove useful citizens to their country and respectable members of society."

- **A.W. Tozer:** "The Word of God well understood and religiously obeyed is the shortest route to spiritual perfection. And we must not select a few favorite passages to the exclusion of others. Nothing less than a whole Bible can make a whole Christian."
- **Billy Graham:** "We are the Bibles the world is reading; we are the creeds the world is needing; we are the sermons the world is heeding."

Be thankful.

Remember that bad things can happen to good people. Can you recall a time of terrible tragedy? Friends and circumstances may fail us, but God never does. Remember that God is in control, and we should keep faith in times of trouble. Trouble in life is not necessarily punishment for our sins. **God is always listening**, and we must trust that He hears and always cares. **Be faithful, be thankful**.

1 Thessalonians 5:18
Be thankful in all circumstances, for this is God's will for you who belong to Christ Jesus.

1 Chronicles 16:34
Give thanks to the Lord, for he is good; his love endures forever.

Colossians 3:15
And let the peace of Christ rule in your hearts, to which indeed you were called in one body. And be thankful.

Psalm 7:17

I will thank the Lord because he is just; I will sing praise to the name of the Lord Most High.

Psalm 107:1

Give thanks to the Lord, for he is good! His faithful love endures forever.

Here in the United States, we are blessed to have Thanksgiving as a national observance, to thank God and honor Him for all He has given us. In reality, as Christians we have something to celebrate in Jesus Christ every day of the year.

What are you thankful for?

Be forgiving.

Philemon, who was a slave owner, was called a fellow worker. He worked closely with Paul. When Paul became a prisoner in Rome, Onesimus, a slave of Philemon, stole from his master and fled to Rome. When Onesimus was in Rome, he crossed paths with Paul and because of their earlier connection, Onesimus stayed and helped Paul and became a Christian convert. When Paul became aware of what was done, he later sent Onesimus back to Philemon in Colossae with a letter and asked Philemon to forgive Onesimus, to take him back as a partner in Christ, and whatever his debt was, Paul agreed to pay it.

Colossians 3:13 NIV

Bear with each other and forgive one another if any of you has a grievance against someone. Forgive as the Lord forgave you.

Matthew 18: 21-22

Then Peter came to Jesus and asked, 'Lord, how many times shall I forgive my brother or sister when who sins against me? Up to seven times?' "Jesus answered, 'I tell you, not seven times, but seventy-seven times.'

Let us not forget the most important forgiveness of all.

Matthew 6: 9-13 KJV

Our Father which art in heaven, Hallowed be Thy Name. Thy kingdom comes. Thy will be done in earth, as it is in heaven. Give us this day our daily bread. And forgive us our debts, as we forgive our debtors. And lead us not into temptation but deliver us from evil: For Thine is the kingdom, and the power, and the glory, forever. Amen.

Who will you now forgive?

Be ready to help and heal where there is a need.

Take some time to resuscitate your faith and show your love to others. Make it a point to read your Bible this week. Spend time and evaluate your own walk with God. Talk with a non-Christian about your faith. You can visit someone in the hospital. Help a friend or neighbor with work. (Your elderly neighbor might need the grass cut.) Go shopping for someone. Take your role seriously as a Christian, plant seeds, and build bridges for Christ!

Acts 1:8

But you will receive power and ability when the Holy Spirit comes upon you; and you will be My witnesses [to tell people about Me] both in Jerusalem and in all Judea, and Samaria, and even to the ends of the earth.

What is your calling and where is your mission?

Christ needs you.
America needs you.
The world needs you.

Help heal our nation!

I believe you can!
Do you?

About the Author

Mr. Burns received a Bachelor of Architecture, a 5-year professional degree, from the University of Kentucky in Lexington, KY, and a Master of Science in Interior Design from UNCG in Greensboro.

He has over 39 years' experience in higher education at Forsyth Technical Community College and has also served as an adjunct faculty at UNCG and Salem College in the Interior Design Departments. In his profession he has received numerous awards for excellence in teaching, and leadership in education, and technology. As an educator, he has created and taught over a dozen new courses relating to architecture, animation, and digital design, and is recognized as an innovator in these fields.

He is a licensed architect in the State of North Carolina, and is known internationally as a guest lecturer for his knowledge and skills in digital design, architecture, sustainability and best business practices in Finland, Belarus, Russia, and Ukraine. Mr. Burns was also a Fulbright Scholar to Russia. He was a member of the first U.S. delegation to complete a certificate of training in Russian business, law, culture, and economics at the Gazprom College of Oil and Gas, Volgograd, Russia.

Mr. Burns has many years of executive business experiences. He is a founding collaborator of the

Center for Design Innovation, Piedmont Triad Design Consortium, Serious Gaming Group, founding collaborator of Design Leadershop, and past president of ABRO Winston-Salem.

Mr. Burns has served as Interim Dean of Engineering at Forsyth Technical Community College, also as Department Chair for Design Technologies, which includes programs of study in Architecture, Interior Design, Radio and Television, and Digital Effects & Animation. He was Program Coordinator for the Digital Effects & Animation Program and served as Coordinator of International Partnerships for the College.

Mr. Burns currently is President of HB Studios in the United States. www.herbburns.com. HB Studios focuses on architecture and interior design, digital content, publishing, international, business, and educational consulting. He is also a host on the popular and international podcast series "Three Men for Thee" https://3-mft.fireside.fm/.

Mr. Burns is an award-winning Christian author. His first two books "Route 66 – Have you found your route in life?" and "Never Stop! Asking, discovering, and sharing" won 5-star awards, and a video award was produced for "Never Stop! Asking, discovering and sharing!" https://www.youtube.com/watch?v=LB IwjqFSxrI&feature=youtu.be. Mr. Burns also created all of the biblical art in the book "Route 66."

If you would like to contact Mr. Burns to speak at your event you can email the request to:

herbburns@mail.com

Acknowledgments

A special thanks to all of the leaders for their contributions to the section "Lessons from Leaders"

Dr. Richard Baxter, Bob Hicks, Nikita Koloff, Alan Cole, Rick Reed, Jack Bales, Anita Teague, Martha Lennon, and Jim Kinney, Tom Burklow.

Resources and references:

The following is a list of web links and the titles used for research and reference.

American history: https://www.loc.gov/classroom-materials/united-states-history-primary-source-timeline/national-expansion-and-reform-1815-1880/

American timeline: https://en.wikipedia.org/wiki/Timeline_of_United_States_history_(1790%E2%80%931819)

American History3: https://www.loc.gov/collections/african-american-perspectives-rare-books/articles-and-essays/timeline-of-african-american-history/1881-to-1900/

Black history: https://en.wikipedia.org/wiki/Timeline_of_African-American_history

Cancel culture: https://www.vox.com/culture/2019/12/30/20879720/what-is-cancel-culture-explained-history-debate

Historical timeline: https://americasbesthistory.com/abhtimeline1940.html

History 1900-1922: https://en.wikipedia.org/wiki/Timeline_of_United_States_history_(1900%E2%80%931929)

History of education: http://www.eds-resources.com/educationhistorytimeline.html

History timeline America: https://en.wikipedia.org/wiki/Timeline_of_United_States_history_(1790%E2%80%931819)

History US Historical Events from 1900 to Present: https://www.baylorschool.org/uploaded/Library_Resources_PDFs/US_History_US_Historical_Events_from_1900_to_Present.pdf

President timeline: https://en.wikipedia.org/wiki/List_of_presidents_of_the_United_States

Promises kept: https://www.promiseskept.com/timeline/

Roosevelt timeline: https://www.infoplease.com/history/us/us-history-progressive-era-and-world-wars-1900-1949

Technology timeline: https://gcn.com/
articles/2007/12/06/25-years--a-technology-
timeline.aspx

Timeline for religion: https://www.pbs.org/
godinamerica/timeline/

Timeline of inventions in America: https://
www.pbs.org/wgbh/americanexperience/
features/telephone-technology-timeline/

US history 2: https://americasbesthistory.com/
abhtimeline1860.html

US history 1920-22: http://timelines.
ws/20thcent/1920_1921.HTML

Vietam war timeline: https://www.history.com/
topics/vietnam-war/vietnam-war-timeline

Education 1776: https://www.businessinsider.com/
school-america-1776-2014-7

First family Adam and Eve: https://truthbook.
com/urantia-book/paper-74-adam-and-
eve#U74_6_2

Definition of family: https://family.lovetoknow.
com/definition-family

3 ways to help your children in a crisis: https:// blog.youversion.com/2020/04/3-ways-to-help-your-kids-adjust-to-the-new-normal/

Six steps for calmness: https://www.theladders. com/career-advice/calm-anxiety-stress-crisis-insomnia

Suddenly Olive tree ministeries: https://myemail. constantcontact.com/Suddenly---In-the-Twinkling-of-An-Eye-. html?soid=1101818841456&aid=nar-k22q-F8